Ecclesia Reformata, Semper Reformanda

Jean-Claude Verrecchia

(Editor)

Ecclesia Reformata, Semper Reformanda

Proceedings of the
European Theology Teachers' Convention
Newbold College of Higher Education
25-28 March 2015

Newbold Academic Press

Editor:
 Jean-Claude Verrecchia
Copy editor:
 Jonquil Hole
Graphic design:
 Any Kobel, Switzerland
Layout:
 CAB-Service, Germany
Typesetting:
 Manfred Lemke
Printing:
 Lightning Source

©Newbold Academic Press, 2016
Bracknell
Berkshire RG42 4AN
United Kingdom
newbold.ac.uk

Except as otherwise permitted under the Copyright, Designs and Patents Act 1988 this publication may only be reproduced, stored or transmitted in any form or by any means, with the prior permission of the publisher, or in the case of reprographic reproduction, in accordance with the terms of a licence issued by The Copyright Licensing Agency. Enquiries concerning reproduction outside those terms should be sent to Newbold Academic Press, Bracknell, Berkshire, RG42 4AN, UK.

ISBN 978-0-9932188-6-6, Softcover
ISBN 978-0-9932188-7-3, e-Book

Contributors

Tom de Bruin, Independent Researcher at the Leiden University Centre for the Arts in Society
(Leiden, The Netherlands)

Reinder Bruinsma, Nederlandse Unie
(Huis ter Heide, The Netherlands)

Laszlo Gallusz, Belgrade Theological Seminary
(Belgrade, Serbia)

Aulikki Nahkola, Newbold College of Higher Education
(Binfield, UK)

Bjorn Ottesen, Newbold College of Higher Education
(Binfield, UK)

Mike Pearson, Newbold College of Higher Education
(Binfield, UK)

Gunnar Pedersen, Newbold College of Higher Education
(Binfield, UK)

Rolf Pöhler, Theologische Hochschule Friedensau
(Friedensau, Germany)

Laurence Turner, Newbold College of Higher Education
(Binfield, UK)

Contents

Contributors	7
Introduction *Jean-Claude Verrecchia*	11
'Ecclesia Reformata Semper Reformanda' – An Urgent Call for Change *Michael Pearson*	17
Who Spoke the Bible? – Orality and the Origins of the Bible *Aulikki Nahkola*	33
Unlearning and Relearning Sola Scriptura – Satan as a Case Study *Tom de Bruin*	59
The Delay of the Parousia – Re-Thinking the Adventist Approach *Laszlo Gallusz*	79
'Revival and Reformation' – A Recent Adventist Initiative in a Broader Perspective *Reinder Bruinsma*	101

Fundamental Beliefs; Curse or Blessing? – On the Pros
and Cons of Adventist Confessional Statements 123
Rolf J Pöhler

Towards a Scripture-Based Theology 149
Gunnar Pedersen

The Church Facing Individualism – A Danish Case Study 179
Bjørn Ottesen

Being Content with Ishmael – A Sermon on Learning from
Abraham's Experience of Learning and Unlearning 199
Laurence A. Turner

Introduction

Seventh-day Adventist European theologians meet every second year for what is called the European Theology Teachers' Convention. This meeting brings together scholars working in the following Adventist institutions Seminar Schloss Bogenhoffen (Austria); Theological Seminar (Marusevec, Croatia); Sazava Theological Seminary (Sazava: Czech Republic); Faculté Adventiste de Théologie (Collonges-sous-Salève, France); Theologische Hochschule Friedensau (Germany); Adventista Theológiai Főiskola (Pecel, Hungary); Istuto Avventista di Cultura Biblica (Florence, Italy); Middle East University (Beirut, Lebanon); School of Theology and Humanities (Podkova Lesna, Poland); Zaoksky Christian Institute of Economics and Humanities (Zaoksky, Russia) Belgrade Theological Seminary (Belgrade, Serbia); Facultad Adventista de Teología (Sagunto, Spain); Newbold College of Higher Education (Binfield, UK). The last meeting was held 25-28 March 2015, at Newbold College. More than 60 participants met around the following theme: *Ecclesia reformata, semper reformanda*. The present volume brings together most of the papers presented during this convention.

The origin of the sentence in Latin is somewhat murky. But it can surely be associated with the Protestant Reformation. Later, Karl Barth referred to it more than once, even claiming that the dynamic *reformanda* should be preferred to the more static *reformata*. Whatever its origin and precise meaning, the sentence is still used as a motto for Presbyterian and/or Reformed churches today.

One may wonder why a Seventh-day Adventist group of scholars decided to spend 4 days around this theme. The reason is that since 2010, *reformation and revival* have become crucial words in the church vocabulary, two leading principles which should sustain its thinking and mission at any level. The question raised is therefore the following: What is the task and responsibility of the church's *didaskaloi* in this process of constant *aggiornamento*?

Ellen White, the Adventist pioneer whose role is still prominent in this church, opened a challenging way with the following words: "we have many lessons to learn, and many, many to unlearn" (*Review and Herald, 26/07/1892*). The actualisation and application of this comment for today's Adventist lecturers lead to the following questions: What do they have to learn and to unlearn in the fields of Biblical studies, Systematics, and Pastoral theology? What should be the leading methodological principles at work in this on-going and never-ending process of reformation and revival? The challenge of this meeting was to explore and discuss new ways of considering theology that could make the best contribution for this church in its specific European context.

In his keynote address, *An Urgent Call for Change*, **Michael Pearson** clearly underlines that the theme of the conference is potentially explosive, as it is designed to disturb religious ideas and professional practices. He also mentions that putting the *didaskaloi* at the centre of the reformation and revival process is somewhat unusual, as there is the temptation in this church to let it be driven by managers. Pearson challenged the audience with the task of 'fishing from the other side of the boat.'

Aulikki Nahkola – *Who spoke the Bible?* – assumes that at least some writings of the Old Testament have been orally composed and transmitted before becoming recorded in the written work. After having looked at how the ideas about the presumed oral origins of the Bible have developed in biblical scholarship over the last century, the chapter addresses the threat(s) or the reward(s) that the acceptance of the oral composition of parts of the Old Testament might present to the Seventh-day Adventist approach to the Bible.

Tom de Bruin – *Unlearning and Relearning Sola Scriptura: Satan as a Case Study* – discusses the role of the Sola Scriptura principle and its correct interpretation. Contrary to most studies on this issue, de Bruin tackles it from a Biblical studies perspective. Far from a theoretical development, he centres his analysis on the interpretation of the role of Satan in Luke 22, with a significant use of extra-biblical writings. He urges the church to learn and re-learn the value of extra-canonical books for a sound and relevant interpretation of the Bible.

Laszlo Gallusz – *The Delay of the Parousia: Re-Thinking the Adventist Approach* – considers that one of the greatest difficulties concerning the *parousia* is the question of its delay. For Adventist authors, this delay is long, faith-testing, even embarrassing. Gallusz critically assesses most of the Adventist attempts to solve the tension. He calls for a hermeneutical reorientation, a clear departure from 'newspaper exegesis' to an understanding of eschatology which helps the believer to live responsibly in today's world. The distance between the cross and the *parousia* 'is not be measured chronologically or spatially, but by such concerns as the realization of God's plan.'

Reinder Bruinsma – *'Revival and Reformation': A Recent Adventist Initiative in a Broader Perspective* – reminds us that the concept of revival and reformation is not a recent invention. This chapter provides the necessary historical background, tracing the origin of the concept back to precursors such as Wycliffe and Jan Hus. Bruinsma critically assesses the previous attempts to achieve revival and reformation within the Seventh-day Adventist church and raises important questions concerning the present situation.

Rolf J. Pöhler – *Fundamental Beliefs: Curse or Blessing? On the Pros and Cons of Adventist Confessional Statements*, tackles an important issue within Adventism. From their beginnings in the 1840s, Seventh-day Adventists denied the need for a creed, as it would hamper the continuous need of further exploration of Scripture. But today's situation is somewhat different as the *28 Fundamental Beliefs* voted and accepted by the church nearly assume the function of a creed. Pöhler examines the reasons for this development. He claims that the church needs to steer clear of the Scylla of dogmatic indifferentism and relativism as well as the Charybdis of creedalism and dogmatic fixation.

Gunnar Pedersen – *Towards a Scripture Based Theology* – notes that despite the Reformers' focus on the Scriptures as the *norma normata*, they failed to fully resolve the hermeneutical question of how to let Scripture be its own interpreter. Pedersen believes that a canonically based Systematics is the response to this hermeneutical deficit. The main task of Systematics is therefore to provide a biblical metanarrative or worldview and to utilise it to assess any belief or confessional article.

Bjorn Ottesen – *The Church Facing Individualism: A Danish Case Study* – presents the most significant outcomes of his research in Danish society. He notes that there is seemingly an irreducible tension between a society for which to find one's genuine self is for many the most important quest and the church for which Jesus Christ and the Bible are the only authorities. Strong individualism is key to Danish society. It creates a pluralistic society, which in a vicious circle encourages more individualism. This is clearly a challenge to mission not only in Denmark, but also in whole Europe. Unless, the church understands this phenomenon and integrates it into its strategy, it might disappear.

Laurence A. Turner – *Being Content with Ishmael: A Sermon on Learning from Abraham's Experience of Learning and Unlearning.* The European Theology Teachers' Convention concluded with a time of worship and spiritual celebration. Turner considers the life of Abraham, to whom God gave the promise that he would make of him a great nation. Abraham thought that Lot would be his descendant. He was not. Then he thought Ishmael would be the son. He was not. Isaac was the son, the only son of the promise. But then, Abraham was asked to go and to offer him... Different learning experiences indeed. Things to learn and to unlearn. '... like Abraham, we need to learn how not to be content with Ishmael.'

Newbold Academic Press is proud to offer these contributions not only to the participants of ETTC, but also to their Adventist colleagues around the world, and to the larger audience of theological academia, beyond its own denominational borders. Whatever the theological differences, there is hopefully the conviction that this 21st century calls for any *didaskaloi* to fish from the other side of the boat.

Jean-Claude Verrecchia

'Ecclesia Reformata Semper Reformanda'
An Urgent Call for Change

Michael Pearson

Introduction – the Call for Papers

The quotation which provides the theme of the conference suggests an agenda which could scarcely be described as 'hidden'. The sub-title dispels any doubt which may linger. If a church wishes to sustain a claim to be reformed it must submit to a continuous process of reform. So this 'urgent call for change' is directed to the teachers who mould the rising generations of pastors and informed lay members, and who thus will inevitably play a significant part in shaping the life of this community of faith. Change of this sort is rarely comfortable and cannot be precisely choreographed.

The theme is provided in Latin, not a language in which Adventists often operate: *'Ecclesia reformata semper reformanda'*. Latin is one of four languages used in the original call for papers. This already suggests that we are to cast our nets wide. Furthermore, Latin is the language of a communion of which Adventists have been traditionally suspicious. So perhaps we are not only to cast our nets wide but 'on the other side of the boat' – as Jesus ordered his own disciples – so as to get the best catch.

So our subject might be rendered: 'A reformed church always needing to seek reform'. Certainly we are 'reformed' in the sense that we are in the extended family of the magisterial Reformation. Certainly we are reformed in the sense that our Adventist forebears felt the need to reform the Reformation in the mid-nineteenth century. But Karl Barth used this phrase, *ecclesia reformata semper reformanda*' in 1947 to urge the church to re-examine itself continually so as to be true to its commission both in doctrine and practice, though the original idea predates Barth by a long way. We are to consider the business of reforming that which some may well believe has no further need of being reformed.

But then I immediately detect a danger. The primary reference in the theme is to 'the church'. I suspect that we find it much easier to talk to each other and to our students about the sometimes bewildering behaviour of the church than the sometimes bewildering behaviour of God. This title, this conference, could become yet another evasion of our responsibility as theologians to talk honestly and authentically to each other about God, about God's recklessly and relentlessly loving pursuit of us, and about our bewilderment in the face of the strange ways God sometimes chooses to express that love. I observe that in these conferences, as in our own college departments, we are somehow reluctant to talk together about God. We talk about the church, administrative matters, church politics, doctrine, policy and the God-concept. We talk all around God but seem to avoid talking about our encounter with God for fear ... for fear of what exactly?

Even mission can become an evasion. Since the General Conference Session of the Seventh-day Adventist Church in 2010, 'revival' and 'reformation' have become crucial words in the vernacular of the Adventist church, two leading principles which should sustain its thinking and mission at any level. So at this conference we are to include consideration of our own tradition and the current official expression of its agenda. It is clear that the phrase 'revival and reformation' is laden with meaning but not necessarily shared meaning, not even shared here among ourselves entirely.

It appears to me that our church leaders have made a miscalculation in choosing this phrase on two counts. The first is a lesson of history, namely that the church cannot organise for 'revival and reformation' however hard it tries. 'Revival and reformation' come when individuals, like Tyndale, Wycliffe, Luther, Calvin and so many others, examine their own experience of God and thirst for more. 'Revival and reformation' cannot be part of a religious organisation's strategic plan. 'Revival and reformation' cannot be contained or branded. The second miscalculation is the idea that 'revival and reformation' can be managed and controlled by the central organisation for its own purposes. 'The Spirit blows where it chooses ... and you do not know where it comes from or where it goes' John 3:8. To believe otherwise is in fact to be faithless and cynical.

The call for papers quickly becomes more specific. It asks: 'What is the task and responsibility of the *didaskaloi* in this process of *aggiornamento*?' The word '*didaskalos*' is not lightly chosen; it is the word commonly used to describe Jesus – 'teacher'. Further, according to Paul, to be a '*didaskalos*' is to perform a leadership ministry. So we are to focus on our own practice as Adventist teachers and thought leaders in the spirit of Jesus. But the New Testament idea that teachers should lead the church has been somewhat lost among Adventists. In fact administrators have in many respects supplanted us in that role. The church is often led by managers. Or are we being too self-important to think that we should play a greater part in shaping the life of the church?

The word '*aggiornamento*' points our minds in another direction. An Italian expression meaning 'bringing up to date', it was a key concept in the highly controversial Second Vatican Council. John XXIII announced his radical initiative in 1959 in pursuit of a spirit of change and open-mindedness in the Roman Catholic Church.

Of course many of those early hopes were subsequently destroyed by traditionalists and insiders, and the Roman Catholic Church has continued to suffer many difficult consequences of the refusal of interior reform in the intervening fifty years. Consideration of *aggiornamento* is a clear invitation to us to 'fish on the other side of the boat'.

The call for papers then abruptly switches direction again. There is reference to Ellen White, at the very heart of the Adventist tradition, who is quoted as saying: 'We have many lessons to learn, and many, many to unlearn'.[1] It is a relatively late statement penned during her Australian sojourn and a period of tension with the General Conference leaders as she attempted reform. In this article called *'Search the Scriptures'*, she further says: 'Long-cherished opinions must not be regarded as infallible'. Those who come to the Bible simply 'to prove their ideas right' will continue in error. 'Those who sincerely desire truth will not be reluctant to lay open their positions for investigation and criticism, and will not be annoyed if their opinions and ideas are crossed'. 'Those who think that they will never have to give up a cherished view, never have occasion to change an opinion, will be disappointed.... Disappointments may prove to be the greatest of blessings to us'. 'We must not trust others to search the Scriptures for us. Some of our leading brethren have frequently taken positions on the wrong side.'

As far as our emotions are concerned she called 'upon every minister to put away pride, to put away strife after supremacy.' She recalled how the pioneers 'would weep and rejoice together' as they sought truth. White's article is a powerful plea for reform which in many ways fell on deaf ears, and many leaders still resist the radical implications of her words. Ellen White urged on us the radical importance of 'present truth'. Some seem to have a preference for yesterday's truth.

---

[1] All references in this paragraph are to Ellen G. White, 'Search the Scriptures', Review and Herald, 26 July 1892, pp. 585-586.

If any have thus far managed to remain unclear about the purposes of the conference, the call for papers grasps the nettle very firmly. It poses the question: 'What do we have to learn and to unlearn in the fields of Biblical Studies, Systematics, and Practical Theology? What should be the leading methodological principles at work in this ongoing and never-ending process?' And then our task is given to us: 'Revival and reformation cannot be a mere repetition of the past. *The challenge of this conference is to explore and discuss new ways of teaching theology that would help the church in its specific European context, to develop and to grow'*. The clear assertion is that there is a connection between the way we teach and the health of the wider church, and that we need to find new ways of teaching theology in the European context.

The clear implication of this single page of conference description is that the process of reform is a vital but by no means an easy or comfortable one. It would therefore be false of me to do anything other than recognise all of this in this address. You may find some of what I have to say uncomfortable, as do I. The only comfort I can give you is that I direct it first to myself, and only then to you.

The Modern European Context

We live on a continent which is to say the least in a state of flux. Most of us live in the European Union which is facing serious threats to its continued existence. Its currency is seriously weakened. A state on its eastern borders which would like to become a member has been convulsed by war. To the east of that is a power which is testing EU resolve and threatening a renewal of the Cold War. To the south the shores of our continent receive boatloads of refugees making desperately risky journeys to and across the Mediterranean to find a better life among us Europeans. Too many simply wash up on our shores as corpses. Mass movements of people generally create conditions in which various nationalisms and violence can easily breed.

Populations increase, resources are threatened, identities blurred. Advances in digital technology change the shape of our lives with extraordinary speed. There is a consequent loss of community and so of intimacy. Church attendance is in decline generally though interest in spirituality apparently is not. Our church cannot expect to be untouched by such massive social change. It cannot expect to stand aloof from it, and still have something authentic to say about God to our fellow Europeans. Our church has to rethink itself for God's sake – and we with it.

The Adventist Church in Contemporary Europe

I am not really concerned here about the Adventist Church beyond Europe except to say that many in that wider church really do not understand the particular circumstances of the church in Europe. They tell us, rather ungenerously I think, that we in Europe are failing, maybe even that we are in fact are faithless. And the answer is to send in the US cavalry!

When I was a child the local church paid quite a lot of money for an annual subscription to two children's magazines produced in the USA. I never read them because there was a message as clear as it was unspoken that this had nothing to do with me. I called the one who bore me 'mum' not 'mom' – one single letter sent a very clear message. All the cultural references were to another country, to the USA. I remain in the Church in spite of those magazines, not because of them.

In Europe we now too easily adopt an Adventism which is not even American but a kind of 'globish' Adventism, a one-size-fits-all Adventism. It is not a road that I see our great '*didaskalos*' taking in his efforts to reach out to fellow Palestinians and anyone else who would listen. Jesus spoke in vivid metaphor rooted in the local context. He enjoyed and encouraged intimacy. Intimacy and community stand in tension with globalism. Even though our church in Europe contains representatives from many non-European people groups, we remain in this particular cultural context of Europe. We cannot ignore that. We cannot entirely sacrifice our cultural context on the altar of the fiction of the 'world church'.

Our church in Europe is generally in decline numerically among indigenous peoples, and the vigour of the church has often only been preserved by immigrants. For that we must be very grateful. On behalf of that church we have been teaching students who have become pastors of those churches, pastors who by many common measures have been failing, whatever the church propaganda may say. What we see in Europe certainly does not fit the conventional upbeat propaganda story of 'revival and reformation'. We ourselves have no doubt to accept a measure of responsibility for this though we should not allow ourselves to be overwhelmed by any sense of failure. And it is to that matter that I must now turn.

If things stay pretty much as they are in our colleges they will probably stay pretty much as they are in our churches. Whether we like it or not, we are to be a force for change. If we refuse the role it will be taken over by some others, most likely Adventist extremists. Or maybe there will simply be drift. Any intentional changes may well be uncomfortable. Our question is: will this conference do anything at all to guide and hasten that change?

Our Own Place in our Colleges in Europe

We work in colleges teaching students to take their place in Seventh-day Adventist Church in Europe. The students change every four years; we do not. There are few career opportunities in Europe for such as us. Therefore we tend to stay in one place for a long time or disappear to the USA. Staying in one place is not necessarily a bad thing but it carries clear dangers of sterility, complacency and dullness. The older we get, the longer we are likely to stay in one position, the more resistant we may become to reform. It is more likely that curricula will remain much the same and not respond to changing social realities. We have vested interests in the curriculum remaining the same because we want to teach what we know best in the way we know best. We are highly specialised, highly gifted and highly attached to our routines. The truth is that we would not fit easily into another system, anywhere else but where we are.

Our colleges are inevitably influenced by our paymasters. There is just as inevitably some divide between church administration and college. Often the wider church would like colleges simply to pass on the tradition. Some would even like to police our colleges more closely. The church sometimes becomes disturbed by some things the colleges teach. It was ever thus – in secular universities too. Universities and colleges are there to be questioning, somewhat destabilizing of the present arrangements so that we can create a future worth living for. Administrations are nervous about the reformist tendencies of the church's teachers. But without reform the church slowly dies.

David Clines on 'Reform' in Teaching Theology

I want to begin my suggestions for reform by referring to an article, originally a presidential address, about teaching Biblical Studies, languages and theology, by David Clines, professor at the University of Sheffield.[2] His agenda is very close in some ways to ours, his passion the same. I can only summarise his main points. These alone, if we took them seriously, would bring reform to our departments. You may find this is strong medicine.

Clines says that we must stop teaching Biblical Studies, theology, and languages and start teaching students. In fact our job is not to teach but to ensure that our students learn. For that they must be

---

[2] Journal of Biblical Literature 129, no. 1(2010), 5-29.

active in the research process, not passive receivers of our collected knowledge. We are not in the classroom to transmit knowledge but to foster understanding. We are there to teach skills, not communicate inert knowledge. We are there to facilitate their learning, not their leaning on us as the sole authorities in the room. We must encourage them to seek meaning, not merely engage in remembering our words just until exam time. They are more likely to remember after the exam if they have been closely engaged in the learning experience, if they have been involved in the structuring of that experience, and most importantly if that learning is embedded in their own existing understanding.

Clines wants more responsibility for their learning to pass to the students. The student becomes a researcher, naïve at first but growing, more responsible for their own development, with us there to guide of course but much less willing to supply answers immediately. In fact we will have to leave our cherished role as authoritative supplier of answers if this is to happen. The learning process will become enquiry-based, question-based not answer-based. It is the method frequently used by our *didaskalos*, Jesus, but it is not so much loved by the church. The church prefers to supply answers to questions it hopes people are asking.

If such reform is to work, then we must seriously consider the ways in which our students learn best. They have different learning styles but we probably tend to cater for a limited range of styles. Lectures have many times been shown to be ineffective ways of making learning happen. Some probably learn best in groups but often our whole system is focused on individual learning, even competitive learning.

Inquiry-based learning means that we would have to reconsider the whole learning experience. Teaching would no longer be separated from research. Our grading systems might also need to change. We would have to consider the baggage of assumptions that we personally bring to the classroom. If we took Clines' proposal seriously it might involve us in major changes in our own approaches to teaching and learning, and indeed to our own credo. I believe that the results might be startlingly good. But it means that we would have to trust our students more, empower them more, simply spend more time with them, and incidentally trust each other more.

Honestly I am not sure how we would cope with such reform. I am not sure that the corporate will to change is there. And no doubt some representatives of the church, our paymasters in fact, would want us to catechise students even more diligently, not less. I would like to see a sub-group of this audience to consider Clines' proposals more closely.

Some Paths to Reform

And so let me come to some suggestions for reform. Let us start with ourselves and be strict and honest with ourselves. We are the key to reform in the education of intending pastors, vital to the future of the church. So we must examine our own performance and our own inner experience. There is no prospect of our proclaiming the 'Truth' unless we are in the habit of being truthful with each other and with ourselves. If reform is to start anywhere, it starts here, among us.

An uncomfortable truth is we like our own areas of power. We like places where we are the boss. We like our sense of authority. We do not like to share control of our classroom, even with colleagues, to generate a new dynamic. We have a problem with the exercise of power in our church – like most others. We must confess to a degree of professional and spiritual pride. We do not like to be challenged too frequently, and mostly our students are complicit; they submit to our authority. Thomas Merton, the Trappist monk, said: 'The words of the proud man impose silence on all others, so that he alone may be heard. The humble man speaks only in order that he may be spoken to'.³ I can only plead guilty to this charge. And what of our students? The immature ones want certainty all the time, they want us to exercise authority.

Clines is right. We must teach students rather than subjects. Management of learning requires that the teacher so constructs the classroom environment that learning will take place. We too easily assume that if we speak it will be learnt. The great illusion of communication is that it has indeed taken place. It is a fundamental error committed by those who confuse their role as teacher with their role as preacher. There is huge leakage in our classrooms. Students often do not really learn the substance of what we say even if they can regurgitate it a few weeks afterwards.

A young Adventist said something to me recently which rather shocked me. He said something like this: 'I think that those who teach in theology departments often tend to exhibit a degree of autism'. My first reaction was denial but the more I thought about it the more I thought there was a grain of truth in it. Let us examine that diagnosis.

Actually we theology teachers tend to be quite shy. We sometimes overcome our shyness by climbing on to a platform where we have a clear role, and we do not have to fight for attention, or engage in small talk. On a platform, or in front of a classroom, you can do big talk. That is what is expected of us. But we struggle to model to our students those simple social skills which build community and which are fundamental to successful ministry.

We hide sometimes because we genuinely find it difficult to make small talk, to listen to others, all those small things which create community. To put it bluntly, we may be somewhat short on social skills, the sort of social skills necessary to equip our students to be creators of communities. We must transmit gifts for making community – but do we have them? One of the great social needs

---

³ Thomas Merton, *Thoughts in Solitude* (London: Burns and Oates, 1954) pp. 87-88.

in European society is the creation of communities. So too in the church. We need to create community churches rather than commuter churches, which are what we sometimes have now. We must educate true pastors, not celebrity preachers. We too easily encourage a certain cult of celebrity in our church, I think.

The theme of autism persists. We need more communication and conversation partnering between ourselves in the European colleges. The fact is that we are in our corners, secure perhaps but often lonely. There is no-one to talk to about our hopes and fears for our church and college. There is no-one to talk to about the challenges thrown up to faith by our own academic discipline. There is no-one to whom we can talk without fear of being judged and quietly being disqualified from further appointment. There is no-one to tell that God somehow has temporarily receded into the distance in our own experience.

We often teach technical intelligence. This may be in biblical languages and modes of interpretation. It may be in huge theological systems. It may be in ethical theories. It may be in practical strategies for preaching, evangelizing or church governance. We love our systems. We do not like it when people threaten our systems, our straight lines.

Actually we are good at innovation in limited spheres. We are good at technical innovation. We love IT and 'boys' toys'. We use machines to improve delivery of classes, distance learning, evangelistic programmes. This is well and good until the technology takes over. People often long for someone simply to listen to them, to talk honestly and simply to them. Of course technology has its place in the communication of the gospel and in our current world it is essential that we communicate via Facebook, twitter and other social media but we may get it out of proportion. Why? Because the technology does not make personal demands of us.

We are poor at teaching emotional intelligence. We are poor at that partly because we are afraid of revealing who we ourselves really are, poor at it partly perhaps because our own emotional intelligence is low. We develop our professorial persona and let the students and our colleagues meet it, not our true selves. We become, strictly speaking, hypocrites, mask-wearers. I challenge you to deny it. I confess – I have been a fellow conspirator.

The worst case scenario is that left-brained lecturers teach a left-brained theology to left-brained students who generate left-brained churches which try to speak to a right-brained world. Our students copy us, they want to be like us, in the end maybe they want our jobs! Of course the system fails. We must pay more attention to emotional intelligence and to social skills in the shaping of the modern pastor.

Perhaps we do not know who we are. We are so used to bearing our persona in our college that eventually we lose track of who we really are. In a rabbinical school in London the preparation of rabbis involves two years of psychotherapy. It is based on the simple fact that unless the young rabbis know who they themselves are and how they affect their congregations, they will either create havoc or simply maintain the status quo. Otherwise there is no chance of reformation. I am not advocating exactly the same but I am suggesting that we place much more emphasis on a programme of personal development for students, the development of their self-awareness, and a functioning tutorial system. We have tried to do this at Newbold but with patchy success. We have to model this self-awareness if it is to become embedded in the curriculum.

'You must be born again and again and again' – so says Jesus, the *didaskalos* to the long-time teacher in Israel, Nicodemus. The reforming church, the reforming theology department, will inevitably demand change of us personally. This is hard for us. How shall we personally grow as followers of Jesus, as Adventist teachers, and still remain faithful to our calling? What seems true in the morning of our lives may have become a lie by evening. Many of us would have to confess that our old expressions of faith are not strong enough to bear the weight of our lives as we mature. Have we got stuck? Unknowingly stuck? Maybe even willingly stuck? Hopelessly stuck? The pace of institutional change does not keep up with that of our own personal growth. Our students in time can 'smell' this on us and they will detect fraud unless we can honestly talk about our own spiritual struggles and show our desire to be reborn.

We are largely male teachers preparing largely male students to minister to majority female congregations. It is inevitable that we will not understand many of their needs, that our students will be unable to create healthy, welcoming and balanced communities in modern Europe. The General Conference failed to welcome women to ministry in its vote in July 2015 and it is already clear that there will be serious consequences for the church in Europe among our children's generation, and even our own. Our children live in a world where this sort of exclusiveness is simply a non-sense. Some will leave, some have left already. The Church avoids this reform at its own peril. So we must ask, do we make our classrooms welcoming to our female students or do they secretly remain second-class citizens?

David Clines wants to submit all theological/ministerial students to a so-called 'pub test'. He warns his students that in a pub or any casual social setting they will hear four typical remarks from people about the Bible: 1. The Bible is full of myths 2. The Bible is anti-gay 3. The God of the Bible is an ugly bully 4. If you are studying theology you must be a very religious person. Clines says that you then have about 30 seconds – no more – to engage the people in conversation about the Bible before the subject will return to football! If would-be pastors/and we too do not pass the 'pub test', if they/we cannot talk energetically and in common language about the Bible, says Clines, they/we are not worthy to receive a degree in Biblical Studies. That is quite radical! Clines wants to see part of the curriculum devoted to popular misconceptions about the Bible which will enable students to function well in an informal social setting.

A famous English politician, Dennis Healey, once said that to survive in politics and be a good politician you had to have a hinterland of interests outside politics. He, for example, was a brilliant photographer. Perhaps the same is true of teachers of theology. We need a certain ease in ordinary conversation. We have to be 3-D people and develop other interests. And incidentally football is a start but it is not enough! It excludes more than it includes.

If there is to be change there has to be management of change. Very often we drift into change. Very often we engage in sanctimonious talk about the Holy Spirit bringing change as an excuse for our not being intentional. Let me be clear, I do believe that the Spirit moves in our work and will take us by surprise. But all too often we are forced into change by external agencies and circumstances.

We would do well to consult those who know about managing change. Managing change often involves having difficult conversations which we would rather avoid in the church. In small institutions these can be very difficult. And we would have to overcome our dislike of outsiders interfering in our business. Change is inevitable in our institutions but will it be intentional or mere drift?

We must hope for greater trust between administrators and scholars. They do not trust us because they have a 'show' to keep on the road at all costs, and we with our many questions sometimes appear to create obstructions along that road. And frankly we not trust their managerial style either. It is lonely when the role of *didaskaloi* is downgraded within our church. We teach a gospel centred on trust but how can we do that effectively when the levels of trust among us are sometimes desperately low?

I could say more but in this keynote address by now you will be clear about what key I am singing in. We need to help our students to find the particular key in which they will sing their song to God. Helping them to find their own unique vocation is surely an important part of our job. How do we do that? Have we first found our own authentic voice?

If you take what I have been saying at all seriously you may now be asking the question posed by Nicodemus as he faced the call for radical reform. But how? How can these things be? How can these things be after one is grown old? Jesus effectively said to Nicodemus 'Use your imagination. Imagine coming into life all over again. Imagine being newly born – a baby.'

We are called to re-imagine our work. We are called to reform. Such reform will not meet with universal welcome. Nicodemus was sincere, faithful, steeped in the tradition, resourceful, zealous for the cause – as we are. Yet still Jesus confronted him with the poignant question: 'You are a teacher in Israel and you do not understand these things?'

We dare not ignore it.

Who Spoke the Bible?
Orality and the Origins of the Bible

Aulikki Nahkola

For confessional Christians, the Bible is the 'Word of God' and since the Reformation it has been the only guide for life and doctrine. In this convention our motto is Ecclesia reformata semper reformanda, and we not only reflect on the past reformation, but also ask whether there is anything for us to 're-form' in our understanding of Bible, that is, any new insights to gain. Recent biblical scholarship has suggested that orality – understanding God's word as a spoken word – can bring considerable insights into the dynamics of what we now have as a written text only. However, if any of the writings in the Old Testament had been orally composed and transmitted before becoming recorded in the written work we now have, how would we know? And what difference would such knowledge make to our understanding of how the Bible came to be, or how we should interpret it today?

It is the purpose of this paper to address these questions. I will attempt to do so by, first, looking briefly, in terms of four main approaches, at how the ideas about the presumed oral origins of the Bible we now have in written form have developed in biblical scholarship over the last century or so. After that I will try to address two further questions, namely, what threat(s) might the acceptance of oral composition and/or transmission of parts of the Old Testament present to the Seventh-day Adventist approach to the Bible? On the other hand, what rewards would this type of study bring to our understanding of the Bible and how we read it today?

1. Approaches to Orality and their Application in Old Testament Scholarship

'Oral' is defined in dictionary terms as 'by word of mouth; spoken; not written'.[1] Applied to the Bible or any literature that we now have in written form, the question becomes one of composition and transmission: how were, say, the patriarchal narratives of Genesis, the Psalms, or the prophecies of Isaiah first composed, that is, put into words? Were they told, sung or declared first, or did somebody compose them with a stylus or brush in their hand and then read them to an audience? And were they passed on by narrating, singing and preaching them again, or simply through a written script? And are there some genres that are originally typically oral, rather than literary, and should we take different things into consideration when we read and interpret them?

The overwhelming evidence from the Bible is that the mode of communication – whether between God and his prophets or the prophets and the people (or indeed Jesus in his teaching) was oral, that is, the spoken word. Yet it has taken until fairly recently for biblical scholars to entertain seriously the possibility of the oral origin of parts of the Bible and to begin to reflect on the significance of such an insight. At the same time denominational literature(s), Adventist or any other, still overwhelmingly, even exclusively, think of the Bible in terms of the written word, written expression – and this even as we continue to exalt preaching, the oral declaration of the Word, in our worship services!

Historically in relation to biblical scholarship there have so far been four main approaches to the potential oral origins of some

---

[1] 'Oral', in The Oxford Compact English Dictionary, ed. by Della Thompson (Oxford: Oxford University Press, 1996), p. 700.

of Israel's religious traditions,² that is, the narratives, laws, oracles, songs and proverbs in which the religious inheritance, beliefs and values of God's people are now recorded. None of these approaches originated in biblical scholarship, but all have been interdisciplinary applications from the many sister disciplines that biblical scholars use to deal with cultural, literary, linguistic, psychological and historical aspects of their discipline. Thus as we think about the impact the appropriation of these approaches by biblical scholarship has had, or could have, on the way we read the Bible, we must remember that the validity or otherwise of these approaches must be ultimately established or contested with references to the disciplines where the said methodology originated.³ Moreover, while I will talk about orality in relation to the Bible, the orality of the Bible even where we may be able to suggest it with confidence is so only in terms of 'anterior speech': what we have is oral composition now in written form, better perhaps designated as 'orally-derived'.⁴

A. Oral origins of the Bible seen as 'veiled and inaccessible'

Oral origins of parts of the Old Testament have been assumed from the earliest times of biblical scholarship – Baruch Spinoza, Richard Simon and before them even Ibn Ezra all made allusions to such origins. Some of this may have been simply based on logic: orality preceded literacy in human history, and some biblical traditions are thought to hail from (literally) the dawn of time, hence

---

2   'Tradition' simply means 'a custom, opinion, or belief handed down to posterity esp. orally or by practice' and is not in itself 'secular' or 'pagan', although in a given culture its contents may be so; see 'Tradition', in The Oxford Compact English Dictionary, p. 1099.
3   Besides recourse to the traditional 'allies' of social sciences, oral scholarship now uses a plethora of scholarly disciplines, such as socio- and psycholinguistics, ethnomethodology, sociology of language, educational psychology, philosophy of language, computational linguistics, etc.
4   See Lauri Honko, 'Text as Process and Practice: The Textualization of Oral Epics', in Textualization of Oral Epics, ed. by Lauri Honko, Trends in Linguistics, 128 (Berlin and New York: Mouton de Gruyter, 2000), pp. 3-54 (pp. 6-9).

such traditions would have naturally been composed in oral form. Secondly, the pre-eminence of the spoken word is abundantly clear in the Bible itself: the very first act, creation, takes place by God's spoken word alone and the frequent refrain in prophetic books is 'The word of the Lord came to me, saying...', which the prophet then goes on to proclaim. Similarly, Jesus is never pictured as writing, but teaching and preaching.

However, the post-Reformation/Enlightenment world, in which questions about how the Bible came into being first started to be posed, was a very book-orientated time (with almost magical belief in the authority of the written word) and in any case, before the nineteenth century nobody had thought of any method by which it would have been possible to explore this generally recognised oral past. Although similar interests were expressed by scholars in other fields of ancient literatures, most prominently the Homeric epics, for all scholars interested in the pre-literate stages of their texts, the past was regarded as 'veiled and inaccessible'.[5]

B. *'Discovery' of orality and its incorporation into biblical studies*
Then in the nineteenth century the way orality was thought about changed dramatically. National romanticism and the ensuing interest in various nations' cultural – particularly literary – heritage resulted, often for the first time, in recording, that is, writing down and systematically collecting, epics, songs, fairy tales, legends, proverbs and so on of these countries. The Grimm brothers of Germany were in the vanguard of this revolution, but methodologically scholarship in Scandinavia and Finland proved more important.[6] A new academic

---

[5] For a survey of ideas about orality in early biblical scholarship, see Aulikki Nahkola, *Double Narratives in the Old Testament: The Foundations of Method in Biblical Criticism* (Berlin: Walter de Gruyter, 2001), pp. 23-27.

[6] Such as the Scandinavian and Finnish scholars Axel Olrik, Moltke Moe and Kaarle Krohn. See Nahkola, *Double Narratives*, pp. 134-50.

discipline was born, folkloristics, perhaps unfortunately so named, as 'folklore' to many has the connotation of something fancifully 'made up', something 'fairytale-like', and for a branch of scholarship this gave the impression of a less than rigorous enterprise – which folkloristics was not, any more than the other new humanistic disciplines[7] for whose birth the nineteenth century was responsible. Today the term of choice for the very same enterprise of studying orally originating traditions cherished by a particular people group is ethnography, ethnolinguistics or ethnopoetics.[8]

The second, and so far the most influential, phase in the study of orality in Old Testament studies was launched by Hermann Gunkel, who, influenced by his compatriots the Grimm brothers and the Danish ethnologist Axel Olrik in particular, suggested in his commentary, *Genesis*, published in 1901, that Genesis consisted mainly of *Sagen* (meaning 'that which is spoken or told', that is 'narratives' in the strict sense of the term). Gunkel argued that at the time of writing down, these stories were already 'very old', had 'a long history behind them', but had been passed on with 'incredible fidelity', nevertheless being subjected to 'universal laws of change'.[9] Gunkel thus attributed the differences in the many variants of what he regarded as the same story-base[10] (such as the two incidents of

---

[7] The nineteenth century was the 'cradle' for many of the disciplines we now call the 'humanities', such as sociology, linguistics, psychology, anthropology and of course biblical studies. Most scholars today are eager to distance themselves in terms of academic rigour from the 'surmisings' of their disciplinary ancestors, but this is the benefit of hindsight.

[8] The rise of this discipline is associated particularly with Dell Hymes and his seminal 1962 essay 'The Ethnography of Speaking', in *Anthropology and Human Behavior*, ed. by Thomas Gladwin and Thomas G. Sturtevant (Washington DC: Anthropological Society of Washington, 1962), pp. 13-53.

[9] Hermann Gunkel, *Genesis* übersetzt *und erklärt* (Göttingen: Vandenhoeck and Ruprecht, 1901), cited in Nahkola, *Double Narratives*, pp. 23-29.

[10] Gunkel sees only one incident here, told twice, in manner to a similar variation occurring in the synoptic gospels.

Hagar's flight in Genesis 16:1-16 and 21:8-21) to the inevitability of stories changing in the telling, that is the 'universal laws of change'.[11]

Gunkel's work has at times been treated in a somewhat patronizing fashion, no doubt because of the idyllic scenes he painted about storytelling by the fireside of the early Israelite 'front room' – his context, or *Sitz im Leben*, for the *Sagen* transmission. Also, the translation of *Sage* into English as 'legend' was unfortunate and caused some misunderstandings, as the term 'legend' for the English-speaking audience conjured up images of King Arthur and the like.

Gunkel, however, had his finger on the contemporary folkloristic/ethno-linguistic pulse to an astonishing extent. His understanding of how variants arose in the act of retelling and how there was a definable and traceable pattern to differences, so that one could recover the original composition (*Ur*–form or 'archetype') by comparing all the variants of a story, concurred with the historical-geographic method[12] of the leading folklorists of his time. The concept of authorship in this approach tended strongly towards a collective one, the speaker being perceived as one who articulated the collective heritage or consciousness of the group.

---

[11] The nineteenth century was preoccupied with 'laws' that would govern language, composition and even social interaction. Several such enterprises found their way to the study of orality, the best known of these being 'Olrik's Epic Laws'. They offer a perceptive description of oral narrative composition, but they hardly merit the label 'law'. See Nahkola, *Double Narratives*, pp. 132-42.

[12] The tracing of an *Ur*-form was thought feasible by folklorists in some cases where tens, even hundreds, of variants for the same epic lay or folktale had been recorded. It was argued that the variants differed more as they became separated geographically and in time. This same notion underlines text-critical attempts to establish the autograph of biblical manuscripts with the help of textual 'canons' and has in recent decades also come under attack by new, more eclectic forms of text criticism. See David Alan Black (ed.), *Rethinking New Testament Textual Criticism* (Grand Rapids, MI: Baker Academic, 2002).

This method remained the dominant folkloristic dogma for most of the last century, both in Europe where it originated and in America where it was quickly adopted. It has only recently been challenged by the performance approach and criticised particularly for the devolutionist and diffusionist cultural models,[13] which it is based on, and for offering a 'literary model of [an oral] text'.[14] This approach has been embraced as recently as the 1960s and 70s by scholars such as John Van Seters in his *Abraham in History and Tradition*, and Klaus Koch in *The Growth of Biblical Tradition*, even, belatedly, attempting an application of the oral laws (the latter more successfully than the former).

C. Oral-formulaic approach

In the 1960s and 1970s the oral-formulaic approach surfaced belatedly in biblical studies to a surprisingly low-profile career, with Robert Culley's *Oral Formulaic Language in the Biblical Psalms*. Based on the famous Parry-Lord studies,[15] first in the Homeric epics and then with living Serbo-Croatian traditions, this approach of recognizing pre-prepared formulas as building blocks of oral composition has had a major impact on the study of many oral-derived literatures, from the Homeric epics to Beowulf.

This approach is similar in assumptions to the method Gunkel used earlier in his work on Genesis, but the main sphere of interest here is poetry, rather than narratives. The key sign of orality is the presence of 'conventions' in the text. In Old Testament word pairing, i.e. using similar or opposite expressions, such as 'death and grave (Sheol)' or

---

[13] Thus called it 'Darwinism adapted to folklore', see Jouko Hautala cited in Nahkola, *Double Narratives*, p. 159, and Alan Dundes, 'The Devolutionary Premise in Folklore Theory', *Journal of the Folklore Institute*, 6 (1969), 5-19.

[14] Elizabeth C. Fine, *The Folklore Text: From Performance to Print* (Bloomington: Indiana University Press, 1984), pp. 28-30.

[15] See Albert Lord, *The Singer of Tales*, ed. by Mitchell Stephen and Nagy Gregory, 2nd ed. (London: Harvard University Press, 2000).

'morning and evening' in the same or parallel lines, is an example of such a convention, as in 'For in *death* there is no remembrance of you; // in *Sheol* who can give you praise?' (Ps 6:5), or 'At *evening* time, lo, terror! // Before *morning*, they are no more (Isa 17:14a).

The psalmist would thus have a repertoire of word pairs (phraseological formulae) at his/her disposal (i.e. memory) to use, as well as the traditional structure for a given genre, say lament, and the theme (e.g. oppression by enemies) and though the composition might appear totally extemporaneous, the psalmist would use these ready-made building blocks in the composition. The knowledge and appreciation of these conventions would have been shared by the audience, and besides testing the singer's skills, functioned as 'shorthand' for cultural concepts and values.

This approach was informed from its start by both text analysis and field studies with living oral traditions, and in some measure heralds the now 'high-riding' performance approach. The importance of the possibility of fieldwork cannot be overestimated, as it was now possible to test scenarios previously only posed hypothetically: would a person performing, for instance, an epic do it differently on different occasions – and how differently?[16]

The main criticism that has been levied against the oral-formulaic approach has been the excessive rigidity concerning the formulae used, or the way they were used, but the approach has recently gone through some promising transformations, largely due to the efforts of John Miles Foley, the 'grand old man' of American orality studies.[17] Now known as 'Immanent Art', this approach has recently been successfully applied to the Song of Moses and Miriam in Exodus

---

[16] The answer to this is 'yes', potentially very differently. See Lauri Honko, *Textualising the Siri Epic*, Folklore Fellows Communications, 264 (Helsinki: Suomalainen Tiedeakatemia, 1998).

[17] John Miles Foley, *Immanent Art: From Structure to Meaning in Traditional Oral Epic* (Indianapolis: Indiana University Press, 1995).

15:1-21, and shows how the poem is not just a victory song over pharaoh's armies, but on a deeper level engages in warfare with pagan deities and ideologies – an example of how orality studies can help us to understand better both *what* the Bible means and *how* it means it.[18]

D. Performance approach

Since the 1980s the focus in orality research has turned on the whole performance event. Although work is being conducted on living traditions of many genres – folktales, sacred texts, proverbs, jokes, riddles, gossip, urban legends, both in literate and non-literate communities – by far the most noticeable branch has been the one focusing on epics. This is partly because the epic is generally a lengthy genre accompanied by substantial performance, and because many of them still exist in oral form.

The performance approach has some of its early roots in anthropology and scholars such as Bronisław Malinowsky, Franz Boas, and Edward Sapir,[19] whose work prompted Elizabeth Fine to formulate the 'ethnolinguistic model of text',[20] now the major force in orality studies.[21] So far the performance approach has been applied to the Old Testament only sporadically, unlike in New Testament

---

[18] Julian P. W. Thompson, 'Orality, Formulae, and Ancient Hebrew Poetry: Understanding Exodus 15.1-21 in Light of Oral Formulaic Analysis and Immanent Art Theory' (unpublished MA dissertation, Newbold College in partnership with University of Wales Trinity St. David, 2012), pp. 89-93.

[19] For seminal articles in this area, see Richard Bauman and Joel Sherzer (eds), *Exploration in the Ethnography of Speaking* (Cambridge: Cambridge University Press, 1974).

[20] See Fine, *The Folklore Text*, pp. 21-28.

[21] The 'performance is king', replaced the 'text is king' –approach, as Honko puts it, constituting nothing short of a paradigm shift in the study of orality. See Honko, '*Text as Process and Practice: The Textualization of Oral Epics*', p. 13.

studies, where much more progress has been made.[22] Three elements, or concepts, are key in understanding this approach: the 'mental text', the 'extended text', and the 'context'.

i. Mental text, but no 'master text'

The most significant element of the performance approach is the notion that in oral composition there is no 'original text' or 'master form' from which variants derive and which can then be recovered by variant comparison and text-critical-type principles – such as the historical-geographical school of folklorists, who influenced Gunkel, maintained. Instead, the performer (usually called 'singer', in biblical terms e.g. prophet or psalmist) has a mental text in his/her mind, which is actualised, that is, textualised, at every performance.[23] Every such telling of a tradition, 'oral text' if you like, is then unique, not just varying between different performers, but in the performances of each individual singer.

This absence of a master text does not of course mean that there was no original, or first telling. Of course there was and in cases such as reports of battles that may have had tangible historical consequences (say the fall of Jerusalem), it is possible to locate to an extent the

---

[22] See e.g. James A. Maxey, *From Orality to Orality: A New Paradigm for Contextual Translation of the Bible*, Biblical Performance Criticism, 2 (Eugene, OR: Cascade Books, 2009); Robert D. Miller II, SFO, *Oral Tradition in Ancient Israel* Biblical Performance Criticism, 4 (Eugene, OR: Cascade Books, 2011); Richard Horsley (ed.), *Oral Performance, Popular Tradition, and Hidden Transcript in Q*, Semeia Studies (Atlanta, GA: Society of Biblical Literature, 2006); Bernhard Östreich, *Performanzkritik der Paulusbriefe*, WUNT 296 (Tübingen: Mohr Siebeck, 2012). The website biblicalperformancecriticism.org covers both Testaments.

[23] Textualisation in folkloristics then means 'oral verbalisation' simply setting into words as an 'oral text', not setting into writing, i.e. 'written codification'. See Lauri Honko, 'Preface', in *Textualization of Oral Epics*, ed. by Lauri Honko, Trends in Linguistics, 128 (Berlin and New York: Mouton de Gruyter, 2000), pp. vii-viii. William Schniedewind thus muddies the waters by using the term 'textualisation' for literary codification, see William M. Schniedewind, *How the Bible Became a Book* (Cambridge: Cambridge University Press, 2004), pp. 1-3.

origins of the report in time and place. But in a truly oral culture that original telling is not recoverable. Even if the name of the person who told the story, sang the psalm or delivered the oracle is known, once the echo of the first telling dies down, the story is gone – a situation exceedingly hard for us today to appreciate.

The mental text, then, consists of plot or structure, and its 'unmissable' episodes, persons and places on the one hand, and a variety of stock phrases and formulaic expressions on the other. The mental text is the bank or 'pool' of the tradition for an individual. How it is textualised on a given occasion is dependent on many factors: the singer's circumstances (e.g. memory, the stimuli he/she receives from the audience), while inspiration as biblically understood would count as a 'divine stimulus', exterior to the speaker. In any case, the performance is not a 'recital' of something committed to memory verbatim[24] – although there seem to be some differences between the fixity of different genres. Certain types of religious utterances, incantations, blessings and curses, legal formulas and proverbs, for instance, tend to be much more fixed than narratives, and there is even some evidence that they may be memorised.[25]

Ethno-linguists sometimes liken the mental text to linguistic preparedness, knowing a language or a dialect. Given a plot, the substance to be told, a gifted storyteller or singer can compose as naturally as we speak our mother tongue. In every performance a unique oral text emerges from this mental text. The mental text does not remain constant but changes and grows throughout the performer's life.[26]

Individual as the mental text is, it nevertheless reflects a larger, collective tradition. This tradition, again, is not a master text, but is

---

[24] See Deborah Tannen, 'The Oral /Literate Continuum in Discourse', in *Spoken and Written Language: Exploring Orality and Literacy*, ed. by Deborah Tannen (Norwood, NJ: Ablex, 1982), pp. 1-16 (p. 1).
[25] See Honko, *Textualising the Siri Epic*, pp. 59-60.
[26] Honko, *Textualising the Siri Epic*, p. 94.

seen as a pool or 'a store of thematic, poetic, performative and other traditional models, elements and rules, shared by different singers' – as Honko has described it – from which performers draw, but as a pool it remains 'extra-individual'.[27] Once again in terms of ancient Israel, this 'pool' could consist of, for instance, the promises to the patriarchs, known to their descendants, established phrases such as 'the God of Abraham, Isaac and Jacob', and the covenant and its obligations. These could be thought of as forming, say, a prophet's 'mental text', which is then 'textualised' at every new declaration into a new message, never with verbatim repetition.

The critical change the performance model offers to what has been dogma in variation development from the birth of the folkloristic discipline, as well as central to form and tradition-historical methods, is this lack of a recoverable master text and the denial of predictable, and hence recoverable, transmission.

ii. Extended text, i.e. performance

The oral text is of course never limited to its verbal elements only, that is, its words. The delivery of the oral text is always a 'performance', and this results in what is called the 'extended text'. In the delivery there are the tone of voice, pitch, stress and pause to consider, besides the words. Beyond that there are other nonverbal elements to consider. These may include 'paralinguistic expressions', such as gesture and body movements, use of space, artifacts, such as instruments and ritual objects, and various types of integral action, such as dance or pantomime.[28]

Fortunately the Bible preserves some 'paralinguistic expressions', particularly in relation to prophecy. Ezekiel's sign-acts, or enacted prophecies, where for instance he builds a 'model' of siege-works, lies on his side for a set number of days facing them and eats food prepared in an unclean manner to portray aspects of the coming

---

[27] Honko, *Textualising the Siri Epic*, p. 92.
[28] See Honko, *Textualising the Siri Epic*, pp. 47-48.

judgment against Judah, form the most extended example of such acts, but they also occur for instance in Jeremiah, when he buys a field as a sign that 'life goes on' in Jerusalem, and most disturbingly in Hosea, where he is told to marry a woman of harlotry to symbolise Israel's spiritual adultery.[29]

But beyond such graphic descriptions of enactments, which the Old Testament is fortunate to have, is anything of the 'extended text' recoverable? The pioneering ethnolinguist Elizabeth Fine treats performance as an aesthetic transaction and suggests that at least some of it is recoverable, even for oral traditions that now exist in written form only and may have been so for centuries, through an exploration of aesthetics in general, and a knowledge about the relevant 'aesthetic field' in particular.[30] Folklorists studying performance in the field – that is, recording epics in India, urban legends in Finland, or Meso-American sacred texts in Guatemala – generally agree that there are commonalities in the performance experience that could be projected back to the study of originally oral texts now extant only in writing. Although agreeing on what would be the 'relevant aesthetic field' for Old Testament will be difficult,[31] a field of scholarship – poetics – closely related to performance, offers some hope for the recovery of the 'aesthetic transaction' in the written residue of formally oral texts.

An area of poetics that has recently come under scrutiny from some ethnolinguists and has deeply influenced the poetics of oral/oral-derived texts, is the division between poetry and prose. 'Prose', argues Dennis Tedlock, 'has no real existence outside the written page', but instead it is, as F. Dobbs-Allsopp has observed,

---

[29] See Ezek 3:22-5.5; Jer 32:7-15; Hos 3:1-3.
[30] Fine, *The Folklore Text*, p. 95.
[31] Even the use of contemporary ancient Near-Eastern cultures as analogues to the Bible is regarded as controversial by many. Jeffrey Tigay has championed the cause of empirical models in ancient Near-Eastern studies. See Jeffrey H. Tigay (ed.), *Empirical Models for Biblical Criticism* (Philadelphia: University of Pennsylvania Press, 1985).

'a phenomenon birthed from the technology of writing'.[32] Many ethnolinguists feel that eliminating the whole notion of prose from the study of oral discourse and replacing it with 'measured narration' and 'rhythmic prose' is the start to recovering the original oral poetics of what are now written texts, as classifying texts as prose or poetry reflects western literary notions of these categories, for instance metre being defined on the basis of numbers of syllables, or stress.[33] This attempt to recover these natural rhythms of a language has been called 'ethnopaleography'.[34]

From a biblical point of view the challenge is to reconstruct an ethnopoetic for ancient Israel, which would adequately reflect the orality of texts and the ethnicity of the people, and not our Western sense of literature. However it has long been recognised by biblical scholars that Hebrew 'prose' cannot be delineated from Hebrew 'poetry' by the simple rules of, for example, Indo-European languages. Steven Weizman has actually labelled Hebrew literature as 'poetic prose' or 'prosaic poetry', and may have already shown the way for some recovery of the lost aesthetic transaction.[35]

iii. Context

Folklore in most societies is performed in situations (*Sitz im Leben*) ranging from the most mundane to the most elevated. There are of course genre differences. Generally the more value-laden folklore – epics, sacred texts – seem to be part of some significant event, such as planting, harvesting, hunting, or worship, rather than just told in

---

[32] Dennis Tedlock, *Finding the Center: Narrative Poetry of the Zuni Indians* (New York: Dial, 1972), p. xix; F.W. Dobbs-Allsopp, *On Biblical Poetry* (New York: Oxford University Press, 2015), p. 237.
[33] Honko, *Textualising the Siri Epic*, pp. 32, 47. See also F.W. Dobbs-Allsopp, 'Poetry of the Psalms', in *The Oxford Handbook of the Psalms*, ed. by William P. Brown (Oxford: Oxford University Press, 2014), pp. 79-98.
[34] Dennis Tedlock, cited in Honko, *Textualising the Siri Epic*, p. 49.
[35] Steven Weizman, *Song and Story in Biblical Narrative: The History of a Literary Convention in Ancient Israel* (Bloomington: Indiana University Press, 1997).

a social gathering, although this may be possible. As was indicated earlier with the performance, the verbal element can become quite secondary to the rituals and all the other paralinguistics that take place.

For the contexts where biblical traditions – narratives, laws, psalms, oracles – were delivered, we fortunately have a good deal of information within the Bible itself. For instance, the celebration of the Passover festival was to contain, for ever more, the recitation of the Exodus experience,[36] the sanctuary services must have had their liturgy, now thought to have incorporated many of the Psalms, while a prophet's demeanour as s/he delivered a given prophecy is often recorded in detail.[37]

As for the ideological harmony between the tradition-performer and the community – there has to be a fostering community for an ideologically-laden tradition to survive. However, the community does not have to be the whole nation or a tribe. It can be as small as a family. And interestingly, field studies have again shown that tradition passed on vertically, for instance from parent to a child, remains more conservative than that passed on horizontally – for instance learnt by someone in a market-place. In the Old Testament we often find the community, or at least its leaders, very hostile to a tradition-bearer's – particularly a prophet's – message, yet there must have been a community of, for instance, disciples who received and treasured

---

[36] Exod 12:25-27.
[37] See e.g. Nathan rebuking David, 2 Sam 12:1-15.

a prophet's words and ensured that they were passed on to future generations.³⁸

2. Challenges of the Orality Approach to the Adventist Concept of Scripture

The one real challenge that the concept of orality appears to offer to the Adventist approach to the biblical text is what oral composition and transmission would mean for the concept of inspiration, and consequently, the authorship and authority of the Bible.

A. Concept of inspiration

If one has a rigid, verbal view of inspiration, envisaging the biblical text as only ever existing in its final written form, it having been dictated verbatim to someone who immediately put brush to papyrus, so to speak, the possible existence of oral antecedents to the

---

[38] The discussion of literacy in ancient Israel and its interface with orality, a major preoccupation of much of most recent research, could legitimately be added as the fifth approach here, but is outside the realm of my current study. One of the seminal works, however, in this field is Walter Ong's *Orality and Literacy: The Technologizing of the Word* and for more recent, biblical application, see Ehud Ben Zvi and Michael F. Floyd (eds), *Writings and Speech in Israelite and Ancient Near Eastern Prophecy*, Symposium Series, 10 (Atlanta, GA: Society of Biblical Literature, 2000).

text might indeed be disconcerting.[39] The same would apply to the concept of the text experiencing some changes while it was being transmitted in writing, until its final fixation by the Masoretes.[40]

But the Adventist 'plenary' concept of inspiration is not actually very rigid at all, stressing the fact that it is not the words themselves that are inspired but the people who wrote them, who thus were 'God's penmen, not his pen', as famously stated by Ellen White. She further explains that the Bible 'is not God's thought and expression. It is that of humanity. God, as a writer, is not represented.... God has not put Himself in words, in logic, in rhetoric, on trial in the Bible.'[41] The message is entrusted to human agency, with its restrictions (i.e. language, logic, rhetoric, literary genres) and that is good enough.

In that respect the possible ambiguities that oral composition and transmission might offer to the concept of Scripture are not unlike

---

[39] In the mid twentieth century some biblical scholars of the so-called 'Scandinavian School', such as Ivan Engnell, Eduard Nielsen and Samuel Nyberg, advocated a very high regard for the reliability of oral tradition, arguing at times for practically verbatim oral transmission of biblical traditions, which would have obviated an immediate need for writing a message down. The empirical models they used to arrive at their conclusion came, however, from cultures where lengthy texts were memorised with recourse to a corrective written text, such as is the case with the Quran, and as such do not address the problem of oral transmission as it is traditionally understood. See Eduard Nielsen, *Oral Tradition: A Modern Problem in Old Testament Introduction* (London: SCM Press, 1954), pp. 11-38. For relevant bibliography and an assessment of the Scandinavian School's approach to orality, see Nahkola, *Double Narratives*, pp. 36-46.

[40] The standardisation of the Hebrew text by the Masoretes, which started soon after the destruction of Jerusalem Temple in AD70 with the fixation of the consonantal text, culminated in the last two centuries of the first millennium as vowels and accents were added. The earliest complete manuscript of the Old Testament/Hebrew Bible as we now have it, is Codex Leningradensis, dated to 1008/9 AD. See Carmel McCarthy, 'Text and Versions: The Old Testament', in *The Biblical World*, ed. by John Barton, 2 vols (London: Routledge, 2002), I, pp. 207-28 (pp. 208-11).

[41] Ellen G. White, *Selected Messages: Book One* (Washington, DC: Review and Herald, 1958), p. 21.

the limitations placed on God's word by the fact that it is written in Hebrew and Greek (and a little Aramaic), which as languages have their strengths but also their limitations.[42]

The Bible is also written by people with various degrees of grammatical astuteness, breadth of vocabulary and gifts for eloquence (compare Mark with Luke, anyone with Isaiah) and it is written in a pre-industrialised world and a world with vastly different views on, for instance, human rights, than what most western societies hold today. If none of that worries us, then neither should the fact that the people who first 'spoke the Bible' did so according to the rhetoric and conventions of their language and culture.

Strictly speaking, even to a person holding a verbal view of inspiration, oral composition and transmission should not be a problem. Nobody would argue that the Apostle John did not know anything about the words of Jesus until inspired to write them down in his gospel or that the newly formed nation of Israel knew nothing about their ancestors until its past was revealed to Moses. How the knowledge of their ancestors that the ancient Hebrews would have inherited from their parents differed from what we now have in the Bible can never be established. Furthermore, in the 'high view of Scripture', which Adventists subscribe to, it is the final, canonical form that has pre-eminence and is affirmed in the Sola Scriptura declaration of faith, rather than any conjectural phase of the text and canon's development.[43]

---

[42] Such as the very 'loose' concept of time/tense in Hebrew and paucity of conjunctions – the latter also becoming a characteristic of some Koine Greek writers, such as Mark.

[43] Otherwise we should be anxious about the apparent loss of such prophetic books as those of the prophet Nathan and the seer Gad (1 Chr 29:29), as well as the book of Jashar (2 Sam 1:18).

B. *Authorship and the authority of the Bible*

Related to the concept of inspiration is the issue of authorship. It is felt by some that if we do not know for sure that, for instance, all the words of Isaiah or Moses came from them and no one else, the Bible would lose its authority. This assumes that we know exactly how inspiration works – that only 'writers' were inspired – and also reflects a very western and, in human history, late understanding of authorship – almost, to use a current term, as 'intellectual property'. Authorship in biblical terms is important for the sake of authenticity. Thus the community's – in this case ancient Israel's and later the Christian Church's – acknowledgement of the authoritative and divine origin of a tradition is what matters most. After all, the Bible itself has not preserved the names of the writers of many of the Old Testament books and of most of the prophets it is recorded that 'the word of the Lord came' to them, rather than that they, personally, wrote their messages down.[44]

This is not to say, however, that the psalms, narratives and prophecies in the Bible did not have authors, even if 'anterior speech' is recognised. While at an early stage of orality studies the tendency was to see composition and authorship as excessively collective,[45] with an individual singer or storyteller almost auto-reciting the community's tradition,[46] today's ethnolinguists see this approach as outmoded, based on romantic nineteenth-century notions of nationhood – besides the lack of understanding of what happens in oral composition/performance.

---

[44] For instance, Jeremiah used a scribe, Baruch, while Isaiah and Ezekiel are actually told to write (Isa 8:1; Jer 36:13-19; Ezek 24:2), but this is fairly late in Israel's history, from eighth to sixth centuries BC. See also John H. Walton and D. Brent Sandy, *The Lost World of Scripture: Ancient Literary Culture and Biblical Authority* (Downers Grove: IVP Academic, 2013), pp. 60-72, 87-96.

[45] See Gunkel above.

[46] Thus not unlike the concept of verbal inspiration, with the source of the material of course seen as divine, rather than communal.

With the 'performance' approach the individual author is back in any case – within the limits of the pre-individualistic concept of authorship – with every performance, that is, a 'performed text' having an individual imprint that can be equated with authorship. This thus supports the biblical description of, for instance, the towering prophetic figures who delivered oracles, which their disciples then treasured, or gifted poet-musicians who composed the psalms: for composing and passing on a sacred tradition – 'performing' in orality speak – is not the realm of the many, but of few individuals. While in secular contexts these individuals are seen as simply gifted and hence self-selected (aesthetically 'inspired'), in the biblical context the inspiration is seen as of divine origin and the 'speaker-performers' would be the ones called by God, although within that bracket, of varying talent.

3. Rewards of the Orality Model to Understanding the Old Testament

As the final form of Scripture is what we do have and as it is that which is our rule of faith, why busy ourselves with the potential oral stages of Scripture at all? The answer is: for the same reason that we study the Bible in its original languages and endeavour to acquaint ourselves with the history, culture and thinking of the people of the time so as to understand the text we have now in more depth. In fact, if we can recognise biblical passages as oral, rather than written, compositions, the rewards for insight not only into the biblical world and the mind-set of its people, but into the meaning of Scripture itself, that is, *what* the Scripture means and *how* it means it, are potentially huge.

A. Oral composition, the speaker and the listener

The basic tenet here is that a person in an oral culture thinks and feels differently in relation to words than his/her literate counterpart. This means, firstly, that oral and written compositions are constructed differently. Oral narratives, for instance, as a rule have fewer characters, simpler sentence structures and much less detail than literary compositions. They also make fewer significant points – often only one – than literary compositions and are restricted in what they can allude to from outside the narrative. [47]

Secondly, and perhaps not as obviously, an oral as opposed to a written presentation of a text 'disposes' people differently towards what they hear or read.[48] Thus a listener retains meaning from a story differently from a reader of the same story. Studies in psycholinguistics have demonstrated that while a reader has a better recollection of the actual sentence structures, details and 'verbatim features', the listener retains the gist of the story, that is, its theme and meaning, better. [49] This, it is argued, is because oral language preserves meaning differently from written language. In oral delivery 'the point, intention or significance of the language, the "speaker's meaning" is preserved in the mind of the listener', while the reader retains more

---

[47] An oral genre can be 'imitated' in writing, but a truly literary genre will always appear as such even when delivered orally. For the 'oral register', see Susan Niditch, *Oral world and Written Word: Ancient Israelite Literature* (Louisville, KY: Westminster John Knox, 1996), pp. 8-59.

[48] See Angela Hildyard and David R. Olson, 'On the Comprehension and Memory of Oral vs. Written Discourse', in *Spoken and Written Language: Exploring Orality and Literacy*, ed. by Deborah Tannen (Norwood, NJ: Ablex, 1982), pp. 19-33 (p. 19).

[49] Hildyard and Olson, 'On the Comprehension and Memory', pp. 20, 31-32.

of the actual words and syntax, the 'sentence meaning'.[50] The reader's recall is thus akin to reproducing an 'artefact', while the listener recalls the meaning of the story better, and for longer.[51]

An important part of understanding the intention of the speaker, the 'speaker's meaning', is a kind of an implicit agreement, sometimes labelled as the 'cooperative principle', which the listener and speaker have: the speaker can count on the listener to make the 'conceptual links' which s/he intends and the listener can trust the speaker that what is inferred by the listener is what was meant by the speaker. Thus the text should not contain any hidden meanings or unspoken agendas.[52]

Understanding and applying this might well help us to address problems in narratives that can be regarded as having an oral origin, such as is the case with the debated 'gap' between the two first verses in Genesis 1,[53] which has been posited to accommodate a greater geological age for the earth than has traditionally been ascribed to the creation.[54] It would seem that if a listener heard: 'In the beginning God created the heavens and the earth and the earth was a formless void…', the inference drawn would be that the earth was a formless

---

[50] The listener 'rapidly' exchanges actual words and syntax to 'interpreted meanings', while the sentence meaning is more like the 'literal meaning'. Hildyard and Olson illustrate the difference with a children's argument. Child A: 'My dad is bigger than your dad'. Child B: 'My dad is bigger than your dad'. The sentence/literal meanings are identical, but the intents of the sentences are different – which is what the listener would focus on. See Hildyard and Olson, On the Comprehension and Memory', p. 20.

[51] Hildyard and Olson, On the Comprehension and Memory', pp. 20, 31-32.

[52] Hildyard and Olson, 'On the Comprehension and Memory', p. 21.

[53] The Creation narrative(s) have caught the attention of scholars even outside biblical studies as good examples of oral compositions. See eg Ong, *Orality and Literacy*, pp. 36-38.

[54] See Davidson, Richard M., 'The Genesis Accounts and Origins', in *The Genesis Creation Account and its Reverberations in the Old Testament*, ed. by Gerald A. Klingbeil (Berrien Springs, MI: Andrews University Press, 2015), pp. 59-129 (pp. 87-104).

void in the beginning when God created it. If the speaker had meant that there was a gap between the creation and the 'formlessness', s/he would have said so, as the cooperative principle between the speaker and the listener excludes hidden agendas.[55]

We are often desperate to 'know more' than what a story offers, but if interested in the original authorial intention of biblical narratives, we do well to consider seriously the points made about oral comprehension. The speaker of course also has a whole arsenal of paralinguistics at his/her disposal – tone of voice, facial expressions, movements, music, rituals. The absence of these in biblical narrative may make us miss such features as irony and sarcasm – the contrast between 'the literal and the intended meanings of the words'[56] – suggested for a whole array of stories, such as Elijah goading the prophets of Baal on Carmel (1 Kings 18:27).

B. *Power of the spoken word*

Understanding the power words have in an oral society will help us recover something of the potency of certain biblical formulas and customs, such as pronouncing blessings and curses, which otherwise may strike a modern person as somewhat dramatised or exaggerated. The death penalty stipulated for a person cursing his/her parents is a case in point: 'Whoever curses father or mother shall be put to death' (Exod 21:17).

---

[55] The example Hildyard and Olson use is of a potential accident: 'There was a terrible squeal of brakes. They saw the girl lying dead on the road.' The inference is that the vehicle struck the girl. Such an agreement of course also exists between the reader and the author of the written text, but as the reader's recollection focuses on the statement rather than the intention, there is more room for interpretation. Hildyard and Olson, On the Comprehension and Memory', pp. 20-21.

[56] Shimon Bar-Efrat, *Narrative Art in the Bible* (Sheffield: Almond Press, 1989), p. 210. Bar-Efrat is not dealing with orality as such, but the 'narrative art' he describes to a large extent originates orally.

Ethnolinguists, such as Walter Ong, argue that 'oral peoples commonly, and probably universally, consider words to have great power', even 'magical potency', as for them 'language is a mode of action and not simply a countersign of thought.'57 Anyone who has studied Hebrew knows that the word for 'word' in Hebrew דָּבָר, dābār, also means 'event'.58 Hence cursing your parents amounts to an event – an act of violence – even as much as the deed done.

This same belief in the potency of the word would also explain why Balaam was hauled by Balak, the king of Moab, at great expense from some 400 miles away to what in our minds might just be to say a few 'well-chosen' words over Israel (Num 22:5). But in his ancient setting Balak believed that the curse was as good as the deed done: that Israel camping at his doorstep threatening to invade was as good as vanquished.

Similarly, understanding the potency of the word explains why in biblical times a person's name needed to match his/her character, for the name 'crystallised' the character and was emblematic of a person's life. This also accounts for the emphasis on God's name and the seriousness of the commandment against taking it 'in vain' (Exod 20:7). And again, when Adam named the animals (Gen 2:20), in an oral society that meant 'conveying power over' them – he had got hold of their 'essence' – for, as Ong argues, in an oral society there is 'no sense of a name as a tag'.59

C. Knowledge is what you can recall
In an oral culture 'knowledge is what you can recall'[60] – a sobering thought! This explains why text originally composed orally entails so

---

[57] Ong, *Orality and Literacy*, p. 32.
[58] A point already made by the anthropologist Bronisław Malinowsky, see Ong, *Orality and Literacy*, p. 32.
[59] Ong, *Orality and Literacy*, pp. 32-33.
[60] Ong, *Orality and Literacy*, p. 33.

many mnemonic devices, such as acrostics and word-pairs, and may help us look at the repetitiveness we sometimes encounter in both poetry and narrative in the Bible as something helpful, rather than a cause for tedium. And again, this explains the instructions for the recitation of the Salvation history – as we have already encountered in Israel's departure from Egypt.

The study of orality is still in its earlier stages and its application to the Bible even more so, and while viewing parts of the Bible as originally orally composed will force us to think more deeply about such matters as inspiration, this is not a bad thing in itself, and besides, there are potentially huge insights to be gained from understanding something about the dynamics of its making and finding layers of meaning so far hidden. I hope that what the above has shown is how the message is inextricably linked to its medium, and that we may in fact misunderstand the message, for instance seeing the trees but not the wood, if we do not appreciate the medium. Oral words mean differently and impact their audiences differently than do written words, a fact that should hardly surprise us in our multimedia age and should provide renewed enthusiasm for preaching – using oral principles, of course!

Unlearning and Relearning *Sola Scriptura*
Satan as a Case Study

Tom de Bruin

Seventh-day Adventists claim to embody the strengths of the Protestant Reformation and to be the continuation of this constantly reforming tradition.[1] As such Adventists embrace the Protestant principle of *Sola Scriptura* wholeheartedly.[2] It is thus somewhat ironic that often Adventists are seen to place the writings of Ellen G. White

---

[1] Consider, for example, General Conference president Ted Wilson's frequent statements on this topic, such as: 'Seventh-day Adventists must hold fast to the Bible as our foundation for belief and practice in this world. The Reformation did not end with Luther … it must continue with us'; Mpande, 'Ted Wilson Says: "Reformation Did Not End with Luther … It Must Continue" | Southern Africa-Indian Ocean Division,' n.d., www.sidadventist.org/ted-wilson-says-a%C2%80%C2%9Creformation-did-not-end-with-luther-a%C2%80%C2%A6-it-must-continue/.

[2] The preamble to the twenty-eight fundamental beliefs of Seventh-day Adventist begins with the words 'Seventh-day Adventists accept the Bible as their only creed,' which clearly refers to the Protestant principle of *Sola Scriptura*.

on an equal footing with the Bible.³ In this way Adventists are singled out as preferring *Prima Scriptura* or even of abandoning the *Sola Scriptura* principle altogether.

In this chapter I will discuss the role of the *Sola Scriptura* principle in the correct interpretation of the Bible. In my view, too often Adventists hide behind this principle and apply it incorrectly. Often this principle is interpreted to mean that it is only permissible to study the Bible in the search for theological edification. But this is a misinterpretation. Rather, it should be understood that 'the Bible is fully sufficient for salvation. In other words, everything that a believer needs to know to obtain salvation can be found in the Bible. There are no deficiencies that need to be filled with tradition, additional revelations or announcements of the church.'⁴ *Sola Scriptura* thus refers not to what should be studied by Christians, but what is authoritative for the church and in the lives of Christians.

The incorrect interpretation of *Sola Scriptura* needs to be unlearned, and the value of extra-biblical writings need to be (re-)learned. In order to show the value of this learning, and how this can continue to reform the church, I will give as a case study a discussion of the role of Satan in Luke 22.

---

    ³ The issue of the role of the writings of Ellen G. White has been addressed in the 2015 rewording of the eighteenth fundamental belief. The most important change is the replacement of 'As the Lord's messenger, her writings are a continuing and authoritative source of truth' with 'Her writings speak with prophetic authority and provide comfort, guidance, instruction, and correction to the church.' This change was proposed 'to avoid giving the impression that Ellen G White and the Bible are equivalent sources of truth. It has also been indicated that the term "source" is difficult to translate into some languages without conveying that idea that her writings are like the Bible.'
    ⁴ Tom de Bruin, *Ministry, Mission and Ordination* (Grantham: Stanborough Press, 2015), p. 16.

1. Extra-Biblical Writings

Traditionally Adventists have not put much store on extra-biblical writings. Non-Adventist authors, both ancient and recent, are treated with a moderate amount of distrust by a certain, often more traditional, group of Adventists worldwide. This is a peculiar observation, for clearly the Adventist pioneers could read only non-Adventist authors. How, then, should we deal with these extra-biblical texts? Considering the study and interpretation of the Bible in its original context, I would like to consider ancient non-biblical, yet religious sources.[5] Regarding these there are four observations I should like to consider.

Firstly, there is clear evidence that the Adventist pioneers read, and in some cases even gave authority, to the deuterocanonical books. While in the eyes of a significant number of modern Adventists these books are 'Catholic' forgeries,[6] the Adventist pioneers did study them. Denis Fortin writes, 'Given our current understanding and rejection of the Apocrypha, it comes as a surprise to many Adventists to learn that early Adventists made references to some of these books in their writings.'[7] In a couple of her earlier writings, Ellen White seems to refer to the deuterocanonical books, but these references are either not clearly from her hand[8] or do not clearly refer to the

---

[5] Better known examples include the Deuterocanonical books, the Pseudepigrapha of the Old Testament, Josephus, Philo of Alexandria, the Apocrypha of the New Testament and the Apostolic Fathers.
[6] Consider, for example, http://adventistalert.com/two-canons/canons.htm.
[7] Denis Fortin, '66 Books -- or 81? Did Ellen G. White Consider the Apocrypha an Inspired Part of Scripture?' *Adventist Review*, March 28, 2002, 9.
[8] When James White republished a letter of Ellen White in *A Word to the 'Little Flock'*, either he or Ellen White added references to the Bible and deuterocanonical books at the time of editing. He writes, 'The following vision was published in *The Day-Star*, more than a year ago. By the request of friends, it is republished in this little work, with scripture references, for the benefit of the little flock'; James White and Ellen G. White, *A Word to the "Little Flock"* (Washington, DC: Review and Herald, 1847), p. 13.

deuterocanonical books.⁹ In the time of the pioneers almost all Bibles would have included the deuterocanonical books. James White, among others, refers to the deuterocanonical works 'as a source of information on last-day events.'¹⁰ All in all, it is safe to conclude that the Adventist pioneers had knowledge of these extra-canonical writings, and that some of the pioneers studied these works, if not as authoritative inspired works, then as witnesses to the context of the canonical works.

The second point I would consider is that much of Adventist theology and ideas is founded on early Jewish and Christian writings. For example, Moses' post-death assumption to heaven is described in Josephus's *Antiquities*¹¹ and in the lost ending to *Assumption of Moses*.¹² It was Origen who first associated the dragon of Revelation 12 with the snake of Genesis, and who first gave Satan the name Lucifer (based on Isaiah 14).¹³ The belief in the Trinity, which was

---

⁹ A document portraying Ellen White's vision on January 11, 1850 reads 'I then saw the Word of God, pure and unadulterated, and that we must answer for the way we received the truth proclaimed from that Word. I saw that it had been a hammer to break the flinty heart in pieces, and a fire to consume the dross and tin, that the heart might be pure and holy. I saw that the Apocrypha was the hidden book, and that the wise of these last days should understand it. I saw that the Bible was the standard Book, that will judge us at the last day. I saw that heaven would be cheap enough, and that nothing was too dear to sacrifice for Jesus, and that we must give all to enter the kingdom'; Ellen G. White, *Manuscript Releases*, vol. 16 (Hagerstown, MD: Review and Herald, 1999), 34. There is some debate about the meaning of this statement, and clearly a differentiation is made between the 'standard book' and the 'hidden book.'

¹⁰ Fortin, '66 Books,' p. 9. Consider also the frequent quotations of 2 Esdras and the Wisdom on Solomon in White and White, *Little Flock*.

¹¹ Josephus explains that Moses, as he was instructing Eleazar and Joshua, was hidden by a cloud and he was taken to a hidden valley. This despite the fact that Moses wrote that he had died in his own writings; *Ant.* 4. pp. 325-26.

¹² Johannes Tromp, 'Origen on the Assumption of Moses' in *Jerusalem, Alexandria, Rome: Studies in Ancient Cultural Interaction in Honour of A. Hilhorst*, ed. Florentino García Martínez and Gerard P. Luttikhuizen, Supplements to the Journal for the Study of Judaism 82 (Leiden: Brill, 2003), pp. 330-35.

¹³ *Princ.*1.5.4-5, and 4.1.22. Cf. Henry A. Kelly, *Satan: A Biography* (Cambridge: Cambridge University Press, 2006), pp. 191-207.

greatly opposed by many Adventist pioneers, is similarly founded in extra-biblical writings.[14]

Thirdly, it seems strange that a church so focussed on gaining more light for the interpretation of biblical texts, and on building a continuously better understanding of God and his plan for humanity, would ignore some of the oldest sources of Christian experience. Surely, Christians who had been taught by followers of the apostles would be able to shed some light, if not on Christian teaching, then at least on Christian life, culture and understanding. By examining how the earliest Christians understood salvation, ethics, church, and other such topics we can shed additional light on biblical writings.

Naturally, any findings from non-biblical writings are wholly subordinate to canonical ones. While Adventists proclaim *sola scriptura*, this does not mean that tradition does not play a role. Admittedly, tradition is a loaded term in Adventism as it is strongly associated with the general Christian beliefs in an immortal soul, hell, Sunday observance, and the annulment of the law. But the use of the writings of Ellen White to guide theology, and even to guide practice, is similarly following tradition. Furthermore, Adventist theology, while strongly grounded in scripture, is in line with much Christian tradition – tradition that we have weighed and found to be biblical.

Fourthly and finally, I must note that in recent years more Adventist scholars have been looking *outside* the canon to better understand it. William Shea, for example, examined Azazel in *1 Enoch* and the *Apocalypse of Adam* to help understand the role of the scapegoat in the cultic system,[15] and Jean-Claude Verrecchia makes extensive use of the extra-biblical works in his examination of the

---

[14] Merlin D. Burt, 'The Trinity in Seventh-Day Adventist History' (Biblical Research Institute General Conference of Seventh-day Adventists, 2008).

[15] William H. Shea, 'Azazel in the Pseudepigrapha,' *Journal of the Adventist Theological Society* (2002), pp. 1-9.

sanctuary.¹⁶ Consider also that Newbold College, the seminary of the Trans-European Division, has been teaching a post-graduate class on extra-biblical writings for many years.¹⁷

A strong case can be made that Adventist theology would be enlightened by a closer study of the extra-canonical writings. Examples abound: the figure Melchisedek in Hebrews, the watchers in Jude, the third and highest heaven in 2 Corinthians. Extra-biblical writings can shed additional light on obscurities. Greater understanding of an author's context can help understand the motivation and goals of these ancient Christian authors – the same authors who helped define the contents of the canon in the first centuries of the church. Early interpretations can give additional light to Adventists today.

In order to illustrate the value of the extra-biblical writings, in the following section I will examine, by way of an example, the role of Satan in Luke 22 in the light of extra-Biblical writings. The goal of this is two-fold. Firstly, this interpretation will shed valuable additional light on ancient ideas of the figure of Satan. Secondly, this discussion will show why the examination of extra-biblical writings is useful in an Adventist context.

2. Case Study: Satan in Luke 22

In general, Christians, and especially Adventists, have a monolithic and systematic view of the figure of Satan. He is an irredeemably evil person, working to bring distance between each individual and

---

¹⁶ Jean-Claude Verrecchia, *God of No Fixed Address: From Altars to Sanctuaries, Temples to Houses* (Eugene, OR; Wipf & Stock, 2015).

¹⁷ Newbold College of Higher Education is, to my knowledge, the only Adventist institution teaching a class on extra-canonical books. The student evaluations show that students are all are very positive about the content. Many mention that the course is an eye-opening experience, and would argue that this module should be compulsory. Jean-Claude Verrecchia, 'Interview: Late Second Temple Judaism, Student Surveys,' August 17, 2015.

God. He achieves this through tempting to sin and the introduction of the spirit of rebellion. The eighth Fundamental Belief of Seventh-day Adventists summarises as follows: 'This conflict originated in heaven when a created being, endowed with freedom of choice, in self-exaltation became Satan, God's adversary, and led into rebellion a portion of the angels. He introduced the spirit of rebellion into this world when he led Adam and Eve into sin.' This view of the opponent is based on a systematic reading of various passages in the Old and New Testaments. One must wonder, however, whether this monolithic view does justice to the variety found within the biblical books.

Luke 22 describes Jesus' last night before his crucifixion. The events of this night are narrated in all four of the gospels. In two of these gospels, Satan plays a role in Judas's betrayal of Jesus. Luke places this influence at the very beginning of his narrative, where he introduces the plot to kill Jesus (Luke 22:3). John introduces the devil's influence over Judas at the washing of the feet (John 13:2), and Judas's succumbing to this influence is complete when he receives a piece of bread from Jesus at the last supper (John 13:27). Matthew and Mark give no role to Satan in this narrative.

Luke is the only gospel to include Satan in the narrative for a second time, the foretelling of Simon Peter's betrayal. Focussing on the synoptic gospels, we can see that all three include an introduction before foretelling Simon's threefold betrayal by sunrise. Both Matthew and Mark begin with a quote from Zechariah 13:7 to introduce the topic of desertion. Luke on the other hand has Jesus speak some words specifically to Simon. These words, unique to Luke, give Satan a place in Simon's betrayal, just as Satan had in Judas's.

It should be apparent that Luke's narrative places Satan in a prominent position, especially in contrast to the other gospels. Luke chooses to associate both Judas's and the other disciples' betrayal with

Satan. This makes this passage specifically interesting for the study of Satan.

Satan and the devil in the Gospel of Luke

At the beginning of the passion narrative, Luke introduces Satan into the narrative. We could see this as Satan's 'triumphant' return to the scene after failing in his testing of Jesus in the desert.[18] Clearly Satan has been on the scene in the meantime; a couple of times Satan has been associated with demons (Luke 10:18; 11:18) and sickness (Luke 13:16). A single time, in the parable of the sower, the devil is described as taking the word of God from the hearts of certain people (Luke 8:12). But his role has been quite minor. Now, at the culmination of Jesus' ministry on earth, he returns:

22.1 Ἤγγιζεν δὲ ἡ ἑορτὴ τῶν ἀζύμων ἡ λεγομένη πάσχα. 2 καὶ ἐζήτουν οἱ ἀρχιερεῖς καὶ οἱ γραμματεῖς τὸ πῶς ἀνέλωσιν αὐτόν, ἐφοβοῦντο γὰρ τὸν λαόν. 3 Εἰσῆλθεν δὲ σατανᾶς εἰς Ἰούδαν τὸν καλούμενον Ἰσκαριώτην, ὄντα ἐκ τοῦ ἀριθμοῦ τῶν δώδεκα· 4 καὶ ἀπελθὼν συνελάλησεν τοῖς ἀρχιερεῦσιν καὶ στρατηγοῖς τὸ πῶς αὐτοῖς παραδῷ αὐτόν. 5 καὶ ἐχάρησαν καὶ συνέθεντο αὐτῷ ἀργύριον δοῦναι. 6 καὶ ἐξωμολόγησεν, καὶ ἐζήτει εὐκαιρίαν τοῦ παραδοῦναι αὐτὸν ἄτερ ὄχλου αὐτοῖς.[19]

22.1 Now the festival of Unleavened Bread, which is called the Passover, was near. 2 The chief priests and the scribes were looking for a way to put Jesus to death, for they were afraid of the people. 3 Then Satan entered into Judas called Iscariot, who was one of the twelve; 4 he went away and conferred with the chief priests and officers of the temple police about how he

---

[18] Bovon, for example writes: 'Satan had been forced to retreat (4:1-13), but he had not abandoned his plans. Here he renews the attack in a roundabout way'; François Bovon, Luke 3: A Commentary on the Gospel of Luke 19:28-24:53, ed. Helmut Koester, trans. James Crouch, Hermeneia: A Critical and Historical Commentary on the Bible (Minneapolis, MN: Fortress Press, 2012), p. 135.

[19] All Greek quotes from the New Testament are from NA28.

might betray him to them. 5 They were greatly pleased and agreed to give him money. 6 So he consented and began to look for an opportunity to betray him to them when no crowd was present.[20]
[Luke 22:1-5]

Luke introduces the wish of the priests and scribes to put Jesus to death. Then, as if in reaction to the priests' and scribes' wishes, Satan enters Judas. The use of εἰσέρχομαι is reminiscent of Luke's descriptions of demonic possession,[21] and seems to have little to do with testing or temptation.[22] Luke gives no further reason for Judas's betrayal, his inhabitation by Satan seems to be enough reason for betrayal.[23] After this passage, Luke describes the preparations for the Passover, the last supper, and then a dispute among the disciples about who is the greatest. After this, Luke lets Jesus foretell Simon Peter's betrayal:

22.31 Σίμων Σίμων, ἰδοὺ ὁ σατανᾶς ἐξητήσατο ὑμᾶς τοῦ σινιάσαι ὡς τὸν σῖτον· 32 ἐγὼ δὲ ἐδεήθην περὶ σοῦ ἵνα μὴ ἐκλίπῃ ἡ πίστις σου· καὶ σύ ποτε ἐπιστρέψας στήρισον τοὺς ἀδελφούς σου.

22.31 Simon, Simon! Understand that Satan has demanded you for himself, that he may sift you like wheat. 32 But I have prayed for you, so that your faith may not fail. And when you [*singular*] have turned around, you must strengthen your brothers.[24]
[Luke 22:31-32]

---

[20] All English quotes from the Bible are from the NRSV, unless otherwise noted.
[21] Cf. Luke 8:30, 32, 33; 11:26.
[22] So also Bovon, who claims 'Luke chooses the language of possession rather than that of demonic inspiration'; Bovon, *Luke 3*, p. 135.
[23] Cf. Johnson, who writes 'instead of attributing Judas' act to greed (cf. John 12:6), or entering into Judas' psychology of betrayal (cf. Matt 27:4), Luke starkly credits the adversary Satan'; Luke Timothy Johnson, *The Gospel of Luke*, ed. Daniel J. Harrington, Sacra Pagina 3 (Collegeville, MN: The Liturgical Press, 1991), p. 335.
[24] This translation is the author's.

Simon appears to be representative of all the disciples.[25] Introducing Satan, Luke makes an intriguing claim: Satan has demanded (ἐξῃτήσατο) all the disciples for himself. Satan makes this claim in order to sift (σινιάσαι) them. Apparently Satan has the right to demand people from (what must surely be the only option) God. Jesus seems quite powerless in preventing this struggle, and can only pray that the disciples' faith will not fail. Curiously, the faith that Jesus prays for will benefit Simon's repentance, not the outcome of the sifting.

This last passage raises a few questions about how Luke portrays the role of Satan. Satan seems to have certain rights in demanding people from God, Jesus seems powerless to do anything against that, and Satan has some role in the sifting of people. Comparing this to the systematic view of Satan outlined above, there are some difficulties. Why would God's opponent have the right to claim God's followers, and how could the opponent perform a function (sifting) generally associated with God?

In order to deal with these difficulties, I will examine a number of details regarding this passage more closely: the meaning of the *hapax legomenon* ἐξαιτέω, the use of the rare verb συνιάζω and the sifting metaphor, and the dichotomy between Jesus and Satan. I will first examine these issues inside the canon, later moving on to extra-biblical sources.

2.1 Luke 22 in the Context of the Canon

When we try to find the meaning of ἐξαιτέω, a *hapax legomenon*, in the canon we discover some difficulties. Related verbs do occur in the New Testament and Septuagint, but one must wonder whether the nuance of the meaning is the same without the prepositional

---

[25] See also Bovon, who writes 'Simon Peter is challenged as a person responsible for and/or representing the Twelve. The readers remember that at the transfiguration Luke presented "Peter and those who were with him" [...] In Acts they will discover Peter's leading role'; Bovon, *Luke 3*, p. 177.

ἐξ–.²⁶ Regarding the meaning, from the corpus of Greek literature we know that ἐξαιτέω in the middle voice generally has the meaning of 'demanding for oneself', 'begging for pardon', or 'averting by begging.'²⁷ One could immediately imagine a context for this verb, as Stählin does in the TDNT, 'in the sense that the devil demands the test, as in Job 1'.²⁸ The verb or any cognate does not occur there, but the narrative in Job 1 does show some similarities. A brief look at Job 1 in this regard is illuminating.

In a narrative where Satan, as one of the heavenly beings, is welcome in the presence of the Lord, the Lord asks Satan if he knows Job (Job 1:6-8). Job is blameless in the eyes of the Lord, fearing God and turning from evil (Job 1:8). Satan proposes that Job's actions are not the result of faith, but of the blessings he receives (Job 1:9-10). He suggests that as soon as the Lord stops blessing Job, Job will lose his faith (Job 1:11). The Lord then allows Satan control over, at first, Job's possessions and family, and later, his health (Job 1:12, 2.6).

In this narrative, Satan claims Job for himself. Not in so many words, but it is clearly the case.²⁹ One must wonder, however, whether this can accurately be described as a 'demand.' Unlike in Luke, there

---

26   The closest usage of a cognate is a passage in the Septuagintal version of Esther, where we encounter a very similar construction with the verb αἰτέω. Esther 8:12n reads: 'τὸν τε ἡμέτερον σωτῆρα καὶ διὰ παντὸς εὐεργέτην Μαρδοχαῖον καὶ τὴν ἄμεμπτον τῆς βασιλείας κοινωνὸν Εσθηρ σὺν παντὶ τῷ τούτων ἔθνει πολυπλόκοις μεθόδων παραλογισμοῖς αἰτησάμενος εἰς ἀπώλειαν'. Which the NRSV translates as 'With intricate craft and deceit asked for the destruction of Mordecai, our savior and perpetual benefactor, and of Esther, the blameless partner of our kingdom, together with their whole nation' (Esther 16:13). In this passage it should be clear that Haman, as part of his plot, demands Mordecai and Esther in order to destroy them. The sense here is possibly a legal setting, but clearly with the intent to kill.
27   Henry George Liddell and Robert Scott, *A Greek English Lexicon*, 9th ed. (Oxford: The Clarendon Press, 1940), p. 582.
28   Gustav Stählin, 'αἰτέω, αἴτημα, ἀπαιτέω, ἐξαιτέω, παραιτέομαι,' in *Theological Dictionary of the New Testament*, ed. Gerhard Kittel, Geoffrey W Bromiley, and Gerhard Friedrich, vol. 1 (Grand Rapids, MI: Eerdmans, 1977), p. 194.
29   So also Bovon: 'to be sure, the verb ἐξαιτοῦμαι does not appear here in the LXX, but the reality is there'; Bovon, *Luke 3*, p. 177.

is no account given of another side. No one attempts to come to Job's aid in this setting, by, for example, praying for his faith. In fact, there does not seem to be any opposition in this passage.[30] After the Lord raises the topic of Job's righteousness, Satan raises possible doubts. Wishing to test Job's convictions, he asks for and is given free rein over Job's possessions and health. The outcome of Satan's tests is the proof of Job's loyalty to the Lord. In other words, because of Satan's actions, Job is vindicated. One might wonder if the book of Job portrays Satan in opposition to the Lord.

Therefore, in the only place in the Bible where we can find wording similar to ἐξαιτέω we see an ambiguous role for Satan. In possibly slight opposition to God, but fully in accordance with God's wishes, he tests Job, ultimately proving Job's righteousness. The ambiguity in the portrayal of Satan's role in Job, and the lack of someone on Job's side, makes it hard to draw any strong conclusions to help us understand the narrative in Luke 22.

The second difficulty in Luke 22 concerns the verb σινιάζω and the sifting metaphor. The verb is a true *hapax legemenon* occurring only here. The context makes it clear that we are talking about some sort of sifting or sieving. It is important to note the contrast between the way this sifting is recounted and the other occurrences of 'sifting' in the canon:

> His [the Lord's] breath is like an overflowing stream
> that reaches up to the neck –
> to sift the nations with the sieve of destruction,
> and to place on the jaws of the peoples a bridle that
> leads them astray. [Isa 30:28]

---

[30] Clearly, the Hebrew word Satan means adversary or accuser. This does not mean that Satan is God's adversary; here he is Job's adversary. Also, there is some debate whether Satan should be seen as a personal pronoun (referring to a single adversary: Satan) or not (referring to an adversary in general). Cf. Numbers 22:22, 32 (supernatural adversary), 1 Samuel 29:4; 2 Samuel 19:23 (human adversaries), 1 Kings 5:18 (adversary of unknown nature). See the discussion in Kelly, *Satan*, pp. 13-29.

> For lo, I [the Lord] will command,
> and shake the house of Israel among all the nations
> as one shakes with a sieve,
> but no pebble shall fall to the ground. [Amos 9:9]

There are two strong contrasts between the sifting in Luke 22 and these passages. Firstly, in both of these passages it is the Lord that does the sifting, not Satan. Secondly, the emphasis of the sifting in these passages is the rubbish mixed with the grain, whereas in Luke it is the grain itself. This contrast seems to suggest that while the stress in Isaiah and Amos is on the unrighteousness of the nations and Israel, in Luke it is the righteousness of the disciples. The suggestion is that the outcome of the sifting of the disciples should be the vindication of the disciples. [31]

As for the third difficulty, for the dichotomy between Jesus and Satan there is no analogy in the canon. Clearly there are passages where Jesus and Satan stand off against each other, but not to prove or disprove a third party's righteousness.[32]

All in all, there still remain some serious difficulties in understanding Luke 22:31-32. The role of Satan is unclear insofar as to why he has the right to demand the disciples for testing. The only comparable context, that of Job 1-2, is quite ambiguous. Satan wishes to sift the disciples, but it seems that the emphasis of the sifting is on the grain, not the rubbish.[33] It stands in contrast to Isaiah and Amos, where the emphasis is on the rubbish itself. Jesus opposes Satan, but only

---

[31] The only possible sifting metaphor that comes close to being interested in the grain itself is Luke 3:17. Here there is no sieving or sifting, but winnowing: God uses a winnowing fork to clear his threshing floor, gathering the wheat in to the barn and destroying the chaff with fire. Here too, though, righteousness seems to be the expected outcome.

[32] One might consider Zechariah 3:1-2, where Satan stands as the accuser of Joshua. But in this case there is no one standing opposite Satan. The Lord functions as the judge and Joshua is the accused.

[33] Contra Beale and Carson, who claim that 'Satan's purpose is to preserve not the good grain, but rather the "chaff,"'; G. K. Beale and D. A. Carson, *Commentary on the New Testament Use of the Old Testament* (Grand Rapids, MI: Baker Academic, 2007), p. 384.

in praying that the disciples will withstand the test, not in stopping it altogether. Based on these difficulties and the systematically monolithic view that many Bible readers have, one might easily come to the conclusion that Satan, in opposition to God's plan, is 'trying to unsettle the disciples and cause them to become unfaithful.'[34] Based on extra-biblical sources, I question if this the correct conclusion.

2.2 Luke 22 in the Context of the Extra-Canonical Literature

Let us now consider what extra-biblical sources can add to the understanding of Luke 22. As we examine the first difficulty, the use of the New Testament *hapax legomenon* ἐξαιτέω, I note that this verb does not occur frequently in Jewish or Christian literature. In roughly contemporaneous and preceding writings it occurs once in Philo,[35] once in the *Testament of Benjamin*,[36] and once in the *Martyrdom of Polycarp*.[37] The only text where ἐξαιτέω is used in the context of Satan is the *Testament of Benjamin*.

The Testament of Benjamin

The *Testament of Benjamin* is the twelfth and last book in a collection of testaments, ostensibly originally given by the twelve sons of Jacob, named the *Testaments of the Twelve Patriarchs*. The provenance of this work is a topic of great debate, but the work is, in my opinion, a second century Christian Greek production drawing on earlier traditions and sources.[38] Chapter 3 of the *Testament of*

---

[34] Robert H. Stein, *Luke*, vol. 24, The New American Commentary (Nashville, TN: Broadman & Holman, 1992), p. 552.
[35] *Spec. Laws* 2.239.
[36] *Test. Ben.* 3.3.
[37] *Mart. Pol.* 7.2.
[38] The provenance of the *Testaments of the Twelve Patriarchs* has been the topic of debate. Consider Robert A. Kugler, *The Testaments of the Twelve Patriarchs*, Guides to Apocrypha and Pseudepigrapha (Sheffield: Sheffield Academic Press, 2001), pp. 29-38. Kugler's final conclusion, that the *Testaments* are a Christian production from the late second century, is the strongest. Cf. Tom de Bruin, *The Great Controversy: The Individual's Struggle between Good and Evil in the* Testaments of the Twelve Patriarchs *and in Their Jewish and Christian Contexts*, Novum Testamentum et Orbis Antiquus 106 (Göttingen: Vandenhoeck & Ruprecht, 2015), pp. 3-28.

Benjamin is an exhortatory pericope that follows an examination of Joseph's life. Joseph functions as the ultimate ethical example of a good and holy man.[39] The children of Benjamin, the purported audience of the work, are called to follow Joseph's example by having a good mind.[40] This exhortation is then continued with the introduction of the forces of darkness:

> Φοβεῖσθε Κύριον, καὶ ἀγαπᾶτε τὸν πλησίον· καὶ ἐὰν τὰ πνεύματα τοῦ Βελίαρ εἰς πᾶσαν πονηρίαν θλίψεως ἐξαιτήσωνται ὑμᾶς, οὐ μὴ κατακυριεύσῃ ὑμῶν πᾶσα πονηρία θλίψεως, ὡς οὐδὲ Ἰωσὴφ τοῦ ἀδελφοῦ μου.[41]

> Fear the Lord and love your neighbour. Even if the spirits of Beliar demand you to endure all the evil of suffering, no evil suffering will master you, just as it did not master my bother Joseph.[42] [T. Benj. 3.3]

Introducing the double commandment, a staple of *The Testaments'* exhortation, the audience are reminded that if they keep a good mind no evil will prevail against them. Even as the spirits of Beliar, i.e. demons, demand to test them through evil and hardship, they will be able to remain strong. In the following verses the audience will learn that anyone who loves his neighbour and fears God cannot be struck down by an evil spirit (*T. Ben.* 3.4). The *Testament of Benjamin* 3.3 is a direct correlate for Luke 22:31-32. In both passages the forces of evil demand (ἐξαιτέω) the righteous. In demanding, the evil forces test them with the evil of tribulation (θλῖψις) or sifting like wheat, but they will not fail if the righteous keep a good mind or do not falter in

---

[39] Harm W. Hollander, *Joseph as an Ethical Model in the Testaments of the Twelve Patriarchs*, Studia in Veteris Testamenti Pseudepigrapha 6 (Leiden: Brill, 1981), pp. 65-92.

[40] For a discussion of the role of the mind in the exhortation of the *Testaments of the Twelve Patriarchs*, see de Bruin, *Great Controversy*, pp. 139-160.

[41] Quotations from the *Testaments of the Twelve Patriarchs* are from Marinus de Jonge et al., *The Testaments of the Twelve Patriarchs: A Critical Edition of the Greek Text*, Pseudepigrapha Veteris Testamenti Graece 1 (Leiden: Brill, 1978).

[42] This translation is the author's.

their faith.[43] In other words, the righteous are demanded to endure tribulation, but these trials will not master those of good mind and body. They will be proven righteous.

As far as the sifting metaphor is concerned, there is little additional information to be found in extra-biblical sources. The somewhat peculiar dichotomy between Jesus and Satan is a different matter. In the Jewish work *Jubilees*, we can find an elucidating passage.

Jubilees

Jubilees was probably written in Hebrew in the second century BCE. We have some fragments of it in Greek, from patristic quotations, and complete Syriac, Ethiopic copies. *Jubilees* presents itself as a divine and angelic revelation given to Moses on Mount Sinai. It recounts the history from Genesis to Sinai in Exodus. In chapter 10 an account is given of Noah, his grandchildren and the influences of 'polluted demons' (*Jub.* 10.1).[44] The demons are 'leading astray and blinding and killing his grandchildren' (*Jub.* 10.2). Unlike in Job, it seems that the influence of the forces of darkness is not in order to vindicate the children of Noah. The goal of these evil spirits is clear, they wish to cause the ultimate death of humans through leading them away from God. Noah attempts to intervene with 'God of the spirits' on behalf of his family (*Jub.* 10.3-6), specifically pleading that the Lord does 'not let the evil spirits rule over them, lest they destroy them from the earth' (*Jub.* 10.3). Initially God acquiesces, and speaks to Noah and

---

[43] A less strong analogy can be found in the *Testament of Job* 20. In this passage, from the perspective of Job we learn that Satan had been unable to provoke Job to unrighteousness by the removal of his goods (*Test. Job* 20.1). Then the testament lets Job recount that Satan then asked (αἰτέω) for Job's body to inflict sickness upon him (*Test. Job* 20.2).

[44] Quotations from *Jubilees*, unless noted otherwise, are from O. S. Wintermute, 'Jubilees: A New Translation and Introduction,' in *The Old Testament Pseudepigrapha: Volume 2, Expansions of the 'Old Testament' and Legends, Wisdom, and Philosophical Literature, Prayers, Psalms and Odes, Fragments of Lost Judeo-Hellenistic Works*, ed. James H. Charlesworth (London: Darton, Longman & Todd, 1985), pp. 35-142.

his children 'so that we *[the angels]* might bind all of them' (*Jub.* 10.6), but soon another makes a demand of the Lord:

> And the chief of the spirits, Mastema, came and he said, 'O Lord, Creator, leave some of them before me, and let them obey my voice. And let them do everything which I tell them, because if some of them are not left for me, I will not be able to exercise the authority of my will among the children of men because they are (intended) to corrupt and lead astray before my judgment because the evil of the sons of men is great.' And he said, 'Let a tenth of them remain before him, but let nine parts go down into the place of judgment.' [...] All of the evil ones, who were cruel, we *[the angels]* bound in the place of judgment, but a tenth of them we let remain so that they might be subject to Satan upon the earth. [Jub. 10.7-9, 11]

The opponent, here called Mastema and later Satan, has a chance to make a demand of the Lord. He needs a number of the spirits in order to do his task; without spirits he has no authority over humans. Thus, Satan demands and God listens, a tenth of the spirits remain. Satan's argument seems to be grounded in the unrighteousness, and deserved death, of most humans. Consider another translation of *Jubilees* 10.8:

> [...] for if some are not left me, I shall not be able to exercise over men the authority I want; for these are *destined* for corruption and to be led astray before my judgement, for great is the wickedness/judgement of men.[45]

In this translation it is quite explicit that the wickedness of humankind is so great that they are destined for death; these humans are so evil that there can be no vindication. Therefore, the demons

---

[45] Translation, with added variants, from Robert H. Charles and Chaim Rabin, 'Jubilees,' in *The Apocryphal Old Testament*, ed. Hedley F. D. Sparks (Oxford: Clarendon, 1984), pp. 1-140.

do not so much lead the children into temptation, but rather show that they are wicked by means of temptation. While this may be a fine difference, this difference does respect the text of Jubilees and the context of Jewish writings (including the Old Testament) better. This second part of the narrative is a useful context for the demands of Satan in Luke 22. There is clear dichotomy between God's elect, Moses, and God's servant, Satan. In this view of Satan's role, it makes more sense that Satan can make demands on God. Obviously, he cannot do his job unless he receives the workforce to do it. Similarly, in Luke 22, Satan fulfils his tasks if Jesus or God refuses to let him work. Thus, as God needs to allow Satan to keep one tenth of the demons, he also needs to allow Satan to try Simon Peter and the other disciples, without Jesus intervening.

2.3 Conclusions on the Nature of Satan in Luke 22

As argued in this chapter, the role of Satan in Luke 22:31-32, and also in Job, does not immediately support a traditional systematic view of the figure of Satan. Obviously, with some effort, both of these passages can be made to fit,[46] but perhaps a homogenous understanding of Satan, shared by all biblical authors, is something that also needs unlearning.

With the passing of time, more and more authors saw Satan as a force for evil.[47] But most of the texts about Satan in the Bible, taken by themselves, equally fit into another interpretation of Satan. Here he would be a necessary part of God's plan, testing the faith of believers in order to vindicate or condemn them. It is only in Revelation that it is incontrovertibly stated that Satan opposes God and works against his plans for humanity. Should this text be allowed to influence the interpretation of all others?

Based on the study above, I propose that Luke 22:31-32 should be primarily interpreted as follows: Jesus knows he will die soon

---

[46] Indeed Fundamental Belief 8 includes Job 1 as a source for its systematic theology.
[47] Cf. 1 John 3:8, 1 Pet 5:8, Rev 12:4-9.

and that all events in his life are coming to a head. In light of the narrative of Job, he also knows that if the faith of the disciples will be tested, now is the time. Satan is God's instrument of testing. He tested and vindicated Jesus (Luke 4:1-13) and he demands that he test the disciples too. Satan wishes to sift them like wheat, in order that they may be proven righteous. Jesus and God would never forbid the testing and (hoped for) vindication of the disciples, as it is part of God's plan and purpose. But Jesus does pray that God will help them in their struggles, so that their faith may prevail.

This interpretation does justice both to the text and context of Luke 22. Systematic thinkers will immediately wonder how this interpretation could fit into the larger systematic picture of Satan. Looking at the various extra-biblical sources, one could easily argue that a development takes place in how Satan is portrayed: moving from a proponent to the opponent, a servant to a rebel. The revelation of Satan's true nature takes place, suitably, in the Revelation. In conclusion, I would propose that we need to unlearn the concept that in every text Satan is tempting humans to sin, and to learn that each Biblical author has the right to his own views.

3. Conclusion

Having finished the exemplary discussion of Luke 22, let us return to the discussion at hand: relearning *Sola Scriptura*. This chapter set out to discuss the principle of *Sola Scriptura* and show which incorrect interpretation thereof should be unlearned. I argued that Adventists need to learn the value of the extra-canonical books. Using Luke 22:31-32 as a case study, we elucidated that passage with canonical and extra-canonical sources alike. From canonical sources little could be learned to tackle the difficulties in the passage. Two extra-canonical sources, on the other hand, showed a broader context for understanding these difficulties. The *Testament of Benjamin* showed an example of the forces of darkness demanding people for testing, as did *Jubilees*. *Jubilees* also gave an extended example of why the opponent could make demands on God, and why Jesus could not, or indeed would not, oppose Satan's actions.

In this study some reflections on the nature of Satan according to Luke 22:31-32 were made. The monolithic, systematic view based on the role of the opponent in Revelation was challenged. I argue that this reading of Satan-as-opponent into many different passages should be unlearned, and we should learn to give each biblical author his own voice. Ultimately, the correct interpretation of *Sola Scriptura* and the value of extra-canonical books need to be learned. As shown in the case study, the variety of extra-Biblical sources give a context on which to build the interpretation of the canonical sources. This variety is vital as it sheds light onto nuances that can easily be overlooked when examining only Scripture. Adventists need to learn to read outside of the safe paths, and relearn the true meaning of *Sola Scriptura:* Scripture is the only necessary source for understanding God's salvation plan, not the only source of understanding.

The Delay of the *Parousia*
Re-Thinking the Adventist Approach

Laszlo Gallusz

Hope in the *parousia* is woven into the very substance of the New Testament. It is looked upon as an integral part of salvation-history, an event grounded in past acts of God, towards which human history progresses under divine direction. For the first Christians, this unfulfilled element of salvation-history was a matter of critical importance, since it was believed that it would bring the restoration of the created order, restructuring the world according to the divine order of things.[1]

One of the greatest difficulties concerning the *parousia* expectation is the constant emphasis in the New Testament writings on the nearness of the event. Since Christ did not return in the era of the early church, and has still not come back after two thousand years, it is inevitable that some questions on the matter must be faced. In the last century, with its considerable scholarly interest in eschatology, the question of the delay of the *parousia* and its significance for the development of early Christianity was one of the critical issues in

---

[1] For the centrality of the *parousia* hope for early Christians, see Christopher Rowland, 'The Eschatology of the New Testament Church', in *The Oxford Handbook of Eschatology*, ed. by Jerry L. Walls (Oxford: Oxford University Press, 2008), pp. 56-72.

New Testament studies.² It was widely argued that the early church had to come to terms with the delay, and that this necessitated theological adjustments in light of the cardinal error of expecting Jesus' soon return. In these academic circles, the delay was considered to have been the single critical factor affecting the transformation of early Christian theology. This hypothesis has been successfully refuted as a scholarly myth without historical basis and it has been widely abandoned, since no strong evidence has emerged to support the view that 'Christianity had changed its character, or been put in jeopardy, by the failure of Jesus to return within a generation of Easter'.³ Although the early Christians looked into the future with a sense of living in history's final age, the New Testament documents and the writings of the early church fathers reflect no signs of experiencing a crisis of delay brought about by the passing of time. This was because of a strong conviction that the most important salvation-historical events had already taken place – the crucifixion and resurrection of Jesus, in which the hope of the *parousia* is grounded.⁴

In this chapter I shall examine how Adventism is coping with the problem of the delay of the *parousia* and the importance of dealing responsibly with the issue. At first sight this enterprise may seem like raising the question of the evil servant who says in his heart, 'My master is delayed' (Matt 24:48). However, I shall argue that the Seventh-day Adventist church could gain much by devoting

---

² Jörg Frey ('New Testament Eschatology – An Introduction: Classical Issues, Disputed Themes, and Current Perspectives', in *Eschatology of the New Testament and Some Related Documents*, ed. by Jan G. van der Watt, WUNT, 2/315 [Tübingen: Mohr Siebeck, 2011], pp. 3-33 [pp. 19-26]) considers the question as one of the four most critical categories in the discussions of New Testament texts, along with the following issues: (1) the character of the eschatological view; (2) terminological distinction between eschatology and apocalypticism; and (3) history-of-religions issues.
³ N. T. Wright, *The New Testament and the People of God*, Christian Origins and the Question of God (Minneapolis, MN: Fortress, 1992), p. 343.
⁴ For the eschatological expectations of the early church fathers, see Brian Daley, 'Eschatology in the Early Church Fathers', in *The Oxford Handbook of Eschatology*, pp. 91-109.

significant attention to the clarification of the issue of the delay and the attendant questions it raises. My conviction is that ignoring the matter is costly because the absence of a clear position takes its toll in critical areas such as Christian discipleship, theology and mission.

1. Clarifying the Expression 'The Delay of the Parousia'

The expression *Parusieverzögerung* ('the delay of the *parousia*') was coined by Albert Schweitzer, who used it first in his famous work *The Quest of the Historical Jesus*, published in 1906.[5] While the term 'delay' generally implies only an extended period of waiting for an event until its actual fulfilment in the future, for Schweitzer the expression signified something more. According to his view, the first delay was the non-fulfilment of Jesus' own expectation that the *parousia* would occur within his lifetime. After the crucifixion, the delay became the problem of the early church, which lived in radical expectation of the *parousia* seen as very close at hand. The continuity of history meant an 'impasse in which Christian faith was caught'.[6] This resulted in an all-consuming crisis in the early church that played a dominant role in the formation of early Christianity. For the proponents of consistent eschatology, who follow such an interpretation of early Christian history, the expression 'delay of the *parousia*' evokes the idea of a mistake in calculation. Even more important, the concept is viewed

---

[5] *The Quest of the Historical Jesus*, trans. by W. Montgomery (London: A. & C. Black, 1910).
[6] G. C. Berkouwer, *The Return of Christ*, trans. by James Van Oosterom, Studies in Dogmatics (Grand Rapids, MI: Eerdmans, 1972), p. 68.

as pointing to the cancellation of the return of Christ, evidence that the expectations of the early church are to be de-eschatologised.[7]

In spite of the theological agenda of the proponents of consistent eschatology, the term 'delay of the *parousia*' has been uncritically appropriated by scholars who use it as a technical term with different meanings and different intentions. When employed by scholars professing a high view of Scripture, the expression does not evoke a sense of eschatological perplexity, but instead points to an intermediate period of waiting that, from a human perspective, has turned out to be longer than anticipated. So Adventist authors refer to a 'long' delay,[8] an 'apparent' delay,[9] or a 'nerve-racking', 'faith-testing', even 'embarrassing' delay.[10]

The use of the expression for this purpose is not the most fortunate, since in everyday contexts it tends to take on negative meanings. It can indicate a reluctance to carry out a specific act at a specific time, the non-fulfilment of a deadline or the failure to meet an appointment.[11] As noted by Robert P. Carroll, 'In order to have a delay there must be a specific time or schedule whereby an event, arrival or expectation

---

[7] The scholarly literature on the critical evaluation of the consistent eschatology is immense. The most influential criticism is provided in two works by Oscar Cullmann: *Christ and Time: The Primitive Christian Conception of Time and History*, trans. by Floyd V. Filson (London: SCM, 1951); *Salvation in History*, trans. by Sidney G. Sowers (London: SCM, 1967). For a response on the interpretation of the key New Testament texts used by Schweitzer, see Anthony A. Hoekema, *The Bible and the Future* (Grand Rapids, MI: Eerdmans, 1979), pp. 109-28; Ben Witherington III, *Jesus, Paul and the End of the World: A Comparative Study in the New Testament Eschatology* (Downers Grove, IL: InterVarsity, 1992), pp. 15-48.

[8] Robert S. Folkenberg, *We Still Believe* (Boise, ID: Pacific Press, 1994), p. 9.

[9] Arnold Valentin Wallenkampf, *The Apparent Delay* (Hagerstown, MD: Review & Herald, 1994); Richard P. Lehmann, 'The Second Coming of Jesus', in *Handbook of Seventh-Day Adventist Theology*, ed. by Raoul Dederen, Commentary Reference Series, 12 (Hagerstown, MD: Review & Herald, 2000), pp. 893-926 (pp. 913-14).

[10] Charles E. Bradford, 'Have We Followed a Mirage?', *Adventist Review*, Second Coming Issue, 2 January 1992, 6-8.

[11] On the unfortunate associations with the term 'delay', see Jonathan Gallagher, 'The Delay of the Advent', Ministry, 54.6 (1981), 4-6.

can be known to be late. Without such information it is not possible to use the term "delay".[12] Therefore, since the time of the *parousia* is never stated, it is meaningless to speak of a delay when God's point of view is considered. It is more appropriate to speak instead about a 'time extended',[13] a 'seeming delay'[14] or to employ the term 'delay' only after making clear that it is not associated with the negative ideas it implies in modern contexts and that it signifies an apparent extension of time.

2. Adventism and the Significance of the Problem

Since the birth of the Seventh-day Adventist Church was rooted in the expectation of the imminent coming of Christ in nineteenth-century America, the belief in the *parousia* has always been central to the Adventist outlook. The conviction that Jesus' coming is almost immediate, that it is 'at the door', was for generations the 'mainspring of Adventism'.[15] The strong advent hope created a sense of constant expectation, keen observation of the 'signs of the times' and the habit of seeing links between contemporary events and the 'time of the end'. The hope of the Second Coming is at the very core of Adventism: (1) the self-understanding of Adventism as an end-time movement called by God is closely tied to the Second Coming;[16] (2) Adventist theology developed by the pioneers is expressed in a prophetic-apocalyptic

---

[12] Robert P. Carroll, 'Eschatological Delay in the Prophetic Tradition?', *ZAW*, 1 (1982), 47-58 (55 n.24).

[13] Gallagher, 'Delay', 5.

[14] Rolf J. Pöhler, Continuity and Change in Adventist Teaching: A Case Study in Doctrinal Development, Friedensauer Schriftenreihe, A/3 (Frankfurt am Main: Peter Lang, 2000), p. 86.

[15] For the significance of the imminence for the Adventist eschatological outlook, see W. B. Quigley, 'Imminence: Mainspring of Adventism', *Ministry*, 53.4 (1980), 4-6, 27; 'Imminence: Mainspring of Adventism – 2', *Ministry*, 53.6 (1980), 11-13; 'Imminence: Mainspring of Adventism – 3', *Ministry*, 53.8 (1980), pp. 18-19.

16 See Jon Paulien, 'Eschatology and Adventist Self-Understanding', in Lutherans and Adventists in Conversation: Report and Papers Presented 1994-1998 (Silver Spring, MD: General Conference of Seventh-day Adventists; Geneva: Lutheran World Federation, 2000), pp. 237-53.

framework;[17] (3) the worldwide mission of Adventism has been driven by this forceful motive.[18] A famous hymn by Wayne Hooper correctly expresses the heartbeat of Adventism: 'We have this hope that burns within our hearts, hope in the coming of the Lord.'

While there have been no major changes in the Adventist understanding of the Second Coming,[19] as Jack Provonsha noted more than two decades ago, 'Maranatha, the Lord is coming, does not come as easily to Adventist lips more than a century' or a century and half later.[20] The reality is that Adventism has gradually drifted away from its strong sense of immediate imminence. The expectation of an impending Second Coming has proved more and more difficult to sustain, especially after the 1960s, because a number of prophecies were not fulfilled as expected. Turkey was defeated without precipitating the end of the world. Neither of the two world wars brought about Armageddon. The election of John F. Kennedy, the Catholic president of the USA, failed to result in a universal Sunday law.[21] Because of these apparent failures in prophecy interpretation, many Adventists became tired of the constant whipping up of emotions that had traditionally accompanied current political developments and felt that they could not keep on finding new signs to interpret.

It is well known that the identity of millenarian groups expecting the imminent coming of Jesus is strongly affected by the passing

---

[17] See Rolf J. Pöhler, 'Der Adventismus als Endzeitbewegung gestern und heute: Endzeiterwartung im Adventismus in Geschichte und Gegenwart – Kontinuität oder Veränderung?', *Freikirchenforschung*, 11 (2001), 120-41.

[18] See P. Gerard Damsteegt, *Foundations of the Seventh-day Adventist Mission and Message* (Grand Rapids, MI: Eerdmans, 1977).

[19] Norval F. Pease, 'The Second Advent in Seventh-day Adventist History and Theology', in *The Advent Hope in Scripture and History*, ed. by V. Norskov Olsen (Washington, DC: Review & Herald, 1987), pp. 173-90.

[20] Jack W. Provonsha, *A Remnant in Crisis* (Hagerstown, MD: Review & Herald, 1993), p. 31.

[21] For a historical overview of the development of Adventism's approach to the 'signs of the times' and the matter of 'imminence', see Malcolm Bull and Keith Lockhart, *Seeking a Sanctuary: Seventh-day Adventism and the American Dream* (San Francisco, CA; Harper & Low, 1989), pp. 44-55.

of time. Adventism is no exception; it seems that the main cause of its identity crisis lies in the delay of the *parousia*. From the way Adventist preachers have presented the Second Coming from the very beginning, we might expect to have been in heaven long before now. However, we are still on earth and the questions are natural and unavoidable: 'What happened? Why are we still here?' William G. Johnsson rightly points to this question as a frustrating factor that is 'eating at the spiritual vitals of many Seventh-day Adventists'.[22] The delay also poses a major challenge for the mission of the church and affects its priorities, as noted at the beginning of the 1970s by Gottfried Oosterwal, the leading Adventist missiologist of the time:

> The Adventist Church stands in danger of losing its missionary fervor and true pilgrim nature as a result of the delay in Christ's coming. As a result, more and more issues of leisure and pleasure are becoming a problem in the life of the church and are requiring a disproportionate amount of attention on the part of its leaders and administrators. Such issues, for sure, have always formed part of the church, but they have remained in their proper perspective.[23]

Since the identity and the entire mission of the church are concerned with the matter of the delay, the importance of the question cannot be overemphasised. The problem should not be reduced to the point of having a mere Cinderella status; instead the challenge must be taken up and given a creative and constructive answer. The whole package of questions arising in the investigation of the problem of the delay needs to be handled keeping in mind the insight of Jörg Frey, who notes in one of his recent publications: 'Eschatology is one of the

---

[22] William G. Johnsson, *The Fragmenting of Adventism: Ten Issues Threatening the Church Today Why the Next Five Years are Crucial* (Boise, ID: Pacific Press, 1995), p. 69.

[23] Gottfried Oosterwal, *Mission Possible: The Challenge of Mission Today* (Nashville, TN: Southern Publishing Association, 1972), p. 20.

most "dangerous" fields of New Testament teaching and [...] there is a deep and vital need for sober and critical reflection.'[24]

3. Adventist Responses to the Crisis of Delay

How did Adventism react to the strong challenge of the delay, an issue that penetrates to its very core? In the following section, I shall discuss five different responses – some of which are not mutually exclusive.

3.1. Eschatological burnout

Focusing intensively on the conditions in the world with the intention of determining how soon Jesus will return may easily lead to emotional fatigue. Whenever the latest world crisis or disaster is seen as a 'sign' that the end of the world is at hand, facing disillusionment is only a step away. Overwhelmed by the pressure of the reality that 'God refuses to comply with their scenarios',[25] affected believers may experience a deep crisis of faith in him. Becoming weary of waiting and feeling like losers, they may turn away in disbelief from all prophecy, living a life in which the *parousia* hope no longer makes a difference in any significant way. In trying to cope with their frustration over the delay, people in this group of Adventists tend to become cynical; some even slip into disbelief.[26]

As a church we need to learn a lesson from Aesop's story about the shepherd boy and the wolf. Crying 'wolf' too many times leads to loss of credibility. Adventist disciple-making should not be based on excitement. As Fritz Guy aptly notes, 'Hope is not euphoria; its eagerness is complemented by a patience that gives to hope its resilience

---

[24] Frey, 'New Testament Eschatology', p. 6.
[25] Wallenkampf, *Apparent Delay*, p. 67.
[26] For a more detailed discussion of the phenomenon of 'eschatological burnout', see Wallenkampf, *Apparent Delay*, pp. 65-69; Johnsson, *Fragmenting*, pp. 71-72.

and durability, so that it can survive delay and disappointment without disillusionment.'[27]

3.2. Intensification of the sense of apocalyptic imminence

In spite of the fact that Adventist commentaries on world events had generally proved to be problematic due to changing circumstances, interpretation of apocalyptic signs underwent a revival in Adventism during the 1990s, after a period of relative silence. Major political developments such as the fall of Communism, the new role of America as a world policeman, the strengthening of the influence of the Catholic church and the growth of ideas about globalisation and the establishment of a 'New World Order' in the context of the dawning of the new millennium brought an intensified sense of the imminence of the Second Coming. More recently, the role of Islam in the final events of earth's history has also become a topic of speculation.[28] The books on these topics produced by well-known Adventist authors and evangelists have become bestsellers, revealing that eschatological fever is still part of the Adventist mentality, even in the postmodern world.[29] The delay of the *parousia* is seen by this group of Adventists as a compelling reason for continuing to stoke the engine of apocalyptic excitement. At the same time, some Adventists have started searching for 'signs of the times' within the developments in the church and bestsellers are being produced on the Omega crisis, the shaking and

---

[27] Fritz Guy, 'The Future and the Present: The Meaning of the Advent Hope', in *The Advent Hope in Scripture and History*, pp. 211-29 (p. 226).

[28] Jon Paulien, *The Day that Changed the World* (Hagerstown, MD: Review & Herald, 2002); Tim Roosenberg, *Islam and Christianity in Prophecy* (Hagerstown, MD: Review & Herald, 2011).

[29] Russell Burrill, *The New World Order: What's Behind the Headlines?* (Keene, TX: Seminars Unlimited, 1992); G. Edward Reid, *Sunday's Coming! Eye-Opening Evidence that These are the Very Last Days* (Fulton, MD: Omega Productions, 1996); Marvin Moore, *The Coming Great Calamity* (Boise, ID: Pacific Press, 1997); Clifford Goldstein, *The Day of the Dragon* (Nampa, ID: Pacific Press, 1999).

other topics.³⁰ For authors of this kind the real enemies are not to be found outside the church but within it.

While creating an atmosphere of urgency by intensifying the sense of apocalyptic imminence may spark a revival and lead to heightened missionary activity, the energy derived from constant anticipation inevitably burns out when the excitement is gone. 'Jesus warned against any form of religion which relied heavily upon outward signs. It was this kind of unhealthy dependence on preconceived ideas of how things must happen which led the Jewish leaders to reject the messiahship of Christ.'³¹ Generating false excitement at every corner is not only unbiblical but also irresponsible. A wiser way to expend our efforts is to live every day for the glory of the Lord by advancing his kingdom as if one were running a marathon, not a hundred-metre sprint.

3.3. Focusing on Human Responsibility for the Delay

A widespread Adventist explanation for the delay is the conditional nature of the timing of the *parousia*. This view looks at the Second Coming as being heavily dependent on human behaviour and accomplishment. The main argument of the theory, known as the harvest principle, is that by focusing on their responsibilities Adventists can hasten the return of Christ and 'bring about' the *eschaton*; when, and only when, the harvest is ready, Christ will come to reap it. The chief proponent of this theory in modern Adventism is Herbert E. Douglass, who explains the harvest principle in his two books *Why*

---

[30] Lewis R. Walton, *Omega* (Hagerstown, MD: Review & Herald, 1981); Keavin Hayden, *The Shaking Among God's People* (Hagerstown, MD: Review & Herald, 1994); Joe Crews, *Reaping the Whirlwind* (Frederick, MD: Amazing Facts, 1985).

[31] Steven G. Daily, *Adventism for a New Generation* (Portland, OR: Better Living, 1993), p. 179.

Jesus Waits (1976) and *The End* (1979).[32] Basing his argument mostly on quotations from Ellen G. White,[33] Douglass explicitly claims that Christ will not return until two conditions are met: (1) the development of a particular degree of readiness on the part of God's people, manifested in a mature character, which serves as evidence in the cosmic conflict that God's law can be perfectly kept; (2) the 'finishing of the work' by dedicated and enthusiastic preaching of the gospel to all the people in the world. The two criteria, sanctification and missionary activity, are closely related: the 'finishing of the work' is to be done in the power of the Spirit, which is poured out on those who have made themselves ready.[34] The bottom line is that the end of the world, the coming or delaying of the *parousia*, depends on the success of Seventh-day Adventists.

In spite of its strong tradition in Seventh-day Adventist eschatology, the harvest principle is vulnerable to criticism on several grounds. First, viewed from a salvation-historical viewpoint, God has never waited for the success of any human factor to deliver a mighty act. While he cooperates with human agencies in carrying out his plan, he is consistent in making decisions independent of their achievements, as shown by the flood narrative, the exodus, the return from Babylon or the first advent, of which it is said: 'But when the fullness of time had come, God sent his Son' (Gal 4:4). Secondly, the harvest principle limits the activity and will of God by subjecting Him to dependence

---

[32] *Why Jesus Waits: How the Sanctuary Doctrine Explains the Mission of the Seventh-day Adventist Church* (Washington, DC: Review & Herald, 1976); *The End: Unique Voice of Adventists about the Return of Jesus* (Mountain View, CA: Pacific Press, 1979).

[33] This position also surfaces in the recent *Ellen G. White Encyclopedia* in a short article on the delay of the *parousia* by Douglass: 'Second Coming of Christ, Delay of', in *The Ellen G. White Encyclopedia*, ed. by Denis Fortin and Jerry Moon (Hagerstown, MD: Review & Herald, 2013), pp. 1141-42. For a balanced approach to Ellen G. White's understanding of the problem of the delay, see Ralph E. Neall, 'The Nearness and the Delay of the *Parousia* in the Writings of Ellen G. White' (unpublished doctoral thesis, Andrews University, 1982).

[34] See, e.g., Fernando Chaij, *Preparation for the Final Crisis* (Mountain View, CA: Pacific Press, 1966), p. 84.

on the activity of human beings. The major difficulty with this view is that it ignores God's sovereignty and bounds it by an arbitrary system in which divine sovereignty is subject to a human agency. If humans were in a position to hasten the *parousia* by their efforts in an absolute sense, that would mean endorsing a strong salvation-by-works emphasis. At the same time, the other extreme is also to be avoided: God's foreknowledge should not suggest determinism or any kind of fatalism. We have a part to play, but ultimately God is the Lord of space and time, and he is in charge.[35] Thirdly, if the Second Coming is dependent on human work, what are the chances that the *parousia* will occur? On a practical level, the number of non-Christians in our world who have not heard the gospel is increasing rapidly every day, so the present global situation certainly does not allow for Christ's imminent coming. Thus, focusing on the assumed importance of the human factor sets us up for a failure that will in turn result in an even greater disappointment and frustration. Fourthly, following the logic of the harvest principle, the existence of some generations is the result of the weakness of prior generations: if they had not delayed the advent we would not have had the chance to be born and to inherit eternal life. So, if this kind of reasoning is sound, such generations would be unplanned, existing merely on account of human weaknesses which delayed the advent. Such thinking clearly relegates some generations of God's people to 'second-class status'.[36]

---

[35] Norman Gulley (*Christ is Coming: A Christ-Centered Approach to Last-Day Events* [Hagerstown, MD: Review & Herald, 1998], p. 542) rightly stresses the need for a balanced position: 'Neither God nor human beings have the sole input into the Second Advent date decision. Rather God's foreknowledge took into consideration all of human hastening and delaying and simply fed all the data into His computer (to use an anthropomorphic illustration) to get the appropriate printout date. His advent will, therefore, take place at the best time, in which He takes into consideration both His foreknowledge and human hastening and delaying. Neither solely determines the date, operating in a vacuum as if the other did not exist.'

[36] Gulley, *Christ is Coming*, p. 542. Probably the most comprehensive criticism of the harvest principle is still the work of Wallenkampf (*Apparent Delay*) aimed at lay readership.

3.4. Hermeneutical and theological reorientation

As a reaction to Adventism's earlier obsession with specifying the political details of final events, a new strand of Adventist eschatology started developing in the late 1970s. Refraining from sketching the future in detail, Adventist scholars began to look in a new direction, investigating the meaning and relevance of the *parousia* hope. This new interest brought emphasis on the certainty and meaning of the Second Coming, rather than on its imminence, and introduced a new perspective into Adventist eschatology. The pioneering work in this theological reorientation was Sakae Kubo's *God Meets Man*,[37] which was followed by Samuele Bacchiocchi's more comprehensive book on the same topic.[38] The reorientation was not only theological but also hermeneutical. The contribution of Hans K. LaRondelle in the area of the hermeneutics of biblical prophecy was also of decisive influence[39] since after him scholars like Jon Paulien and Ranko Stefanovic began to focus on the exegetical investigation of biblical texts containing prophetic material, rather than commenting on current events by means of 'newspaper exegesis'.[40] A quite recent development is the in-depth investigation of theological themes in the books of Revelation

---

[37] *God Meets Man: A Theology of the Sabbath and Second Coming* (Nashville, TN: Southern Publishing Association, 1978).

[38] Samuele Bacchiocchi, *The Advent Hope for Human Hopelessness*, Biblical Perspectives, 6 (Berrien Springs, MI: Biblical Perspectives, 1986).

[39] *The Israel of God in Prophecy: Principles of Prophetic Interpretation* (Berrien Springs, MI: Andrews University Press, 1983); *Chariots of Salvation: The Biblical Drama of Armageddon* (Washington, DC: Review & Herald, 1987).

[40] Jon Paulien, *Decoding Revelation's Trumpets: Literary Allusions and Interpretation of Revelation 8:7-12*, AUSDDS, 2 (Berrien Springs, MI: Andrews University Press, 1987); *What the Bible Says about the End-Time* (Hagerstown, MD: Review & Herald, 1994); *The Deep Things of God* (Hagerstown, MD: Review & Herald, 2004); Ranko Stefanovic, *The Background and Meaning of the Sealed Book of Revelation 5*, AUSDDS, 22 (Berrien Springs, MI: Andrews University Press, 1996); *Revelation of Jesus Christ* (Berrien Springs, MI: Andrews University Press, 2002).

and Daniel, which seems a promising direction for Adventist interpretation.[41]

As noted by Malcolm Bull and Keith Lockhart, it is tempting to interpret the shift away from the central concern with the imminence of the Second Coming 'as evidence that the Adventist church has lost its early apocalyptic enthusiasm'.[42] This would, however, be an oversimplification. Moving away from date-setting or almost date-setting mechanisms in generating a sense of imminence is a sign of a mature faith, not the abandonment of our cause.

3.5. Focusing on the healing aspect of the gospel

While eschatological ideas are traditionally central to the Seventh-day Adventist outlook, as a consequence of the delay apocalyptic orientation has started to be counterbalanced, in the last half century, by an emphasis on the healing aspect of the gospel. It has been recognised that future-oriented expectations have to make a difference now on earth and that Adventists must therefore show concern to make this world a better place instead of being pessimistic about it. This concern requires social and political engagement with rejection of retreat from ethical responsibility.[43]

While at times there have been tensions between the streams of thought emphasizing the apocalyptic or the healing aspect of

---

[41] See Sigve Tonstad, *Saving God's Reputation: The Theological Function of Pistis Iesou in the Cosmic Narratives of Revelation*, LNTS, 337 (London: T&T Clark, 2006); Laszlo Gallusz, *The Throne Motif in the Book of Revelation*, LNTS, 487 (London: Bloomsbury T&T Clark, 2014); Steven Grabiner, *Revelation's Hymns: Commentary on the Cosmic Conflict*, LNTS, 511 (London: Bloomsbury T&T Clark, 2015); Paul Birch Petersen, *The Theology and the Function of the Prayers in the Book of Daniel* (unpublished doctoral thesis, Andrews University, 1998); Winfried Vogel, *The Cultic Motif in the Book of Daniel* (New York: Peter Lang, 2010); Ivan Milanov, 'Lords and the Lord: The Motifs of Hubris in Daniel 1-6' (unpublished doctoral thesis, University of Wales, Lampeter Trinity Saint David, 2014).

[42] Bull, *Seeking a Sanctuary*, p. 54.

[43] On Adventist addressing of moral issues, see Michael Pearson, *Millennial Dreams and Moral Dilemmas: Seventh-day Adventism and Contemporary Ethics* (Cambridge: Cambridge University Press, 1990).

the gospel, it has been frequently demonstrated that the emphases on a future-oriented hope and on social responsibility are not mutually exclusive.[44] Since ideas always have practical consequences, eschatology is to be seen as a driving force of ethical engagement.[45] As noted by Brunt, 'The eschatological vision of our future hope actually contributes to the *content* or shape of our daily lives. It helps us see how we should live responsibly here and now.'[46] Overemphasizing either the apocalyptic or the healing features of the gospel leads to a distorted discipleship and thus an unbalanced relationship to the advent hope.

4. How can the Parousia Hope Shine Again as a Blessed Hope?

the above discussion has revealed that the *parousia* hope has often been misused and that for many Adventists it has become a frustrating factor or an event in the distant future, rather than a blessed hope. The deepest root of the problem lies in the problem of delay, which has not received the detailed attention it deserves. While in recent decades the question has begun to be treated as a specific component within Adventist eschatology, attention to it has been scarce by comparison with its significance for the theology, mission and life of the church.[47] From time to time Adventist interpreters have attempted to wrestle with the problem in brief publications, but their arguments have not generally sprung from in-depth study of

---

[44] See, for example, John Brunt, *Now & Not Yet* (Washington, DC: Review & Herald, 1987).
[45] Pöhler, 'Adventismus'.
[46] Brunt, *Now & Not Yet*, p. 16.
[47] For example, only one page is devoted to the question in the *Handbook of Seventh-day Adventist Theology* (Lehmann, 'Second Coming', pp. 913–14) and not much more in the well-known Adventist systematic theology authored by Richard Rice (*Reign of God* [Berrien Springs, MI: Andrews University Press, 1985]).

biblical texts.[48] Their works have most often been mere reflections intended for a popular readership. Indeed, they have been little more than attempts to provide various rationales for explaining the long interim period. In fact, no detailed Adventist scholarly analysis of the problem is available, in spite of the remarkable discussions by such scholars as Arnold Valentine Wallenkampf,[49] Fritz Guy,[50] Rolf Pöhler[51] and Norman Gulley.[52] Interest in the problem of the delay is, similarly, no greater in non-Adventist scholarly circles, where the detailed study by Kurt Erlemann is among rare exceptions.[53]

Since the question of the delay of the *parousia* confronts Adventism – and more widely the whole of Christianity – at its core, ignoring it by marginalizing it is not a viable option. We need an intelligent faith which is ready to face difficult issues, even if the discussions may make some of us nervous or a bit angry. The hope of the Second Coming may regain its motivational force only if persistent questions are raised and answered in a frank and open discussion, treating related issues thoroughly, with the intention of developing a balanced and biblical theology of hope. The repetition of the prediction that Christ's

[48] See Gallagher, 'Delay'; Ralph E. Neall, 'Why are We Still Here?', *Adventist Review*, Second Coming Issue, 2 January 1992, 9-10; Jon Paulien, 'How Long Must We Wait?', *Adventist Review*, Second Coming Issue, 2 January 1992, 16-17; Roy Adams, 'Why are We Still Here?', *Adventist Review*, 150-Year Anniversary Issue, 6 October 1994, 36-38; Mario Veloso, 'There is No Delay', *Ministry*, 69.12 (1996), 6-8; Zdravko Stefanovic, 'Delay? What Delay? Seeing the Impending Advent Through Oriental Eyes', *Adventist Review*, 29 October 1998, 68-70; Richard P. Lehmann, '"How Long, O Lord, How Long?"', in *Exploring the Frontiers of Faith: Festschrift in Honour of Dr. Jan Paulsen*, ed. by Borge Schantz and Reinder Bruinsma (Lueneburg: Advent-Verlag, 2009), pp. 219-24.
[49] Wallenkampf, *Apparent Delay*.
[50] Guy, 'Future'.
[51] Pöhler, 'Adventismus'.
[52] Norman Gulley, *Systematic Theology, vol. 4: Church and Final Events* (Berrien Springs, MI: Andrews University Press, forthcoming, 2015).
[53] Kurt Erlemann, *Naherwartung und Parusieverzögung im Neuen Testament: Ein Beitrag zur religiöser Zeiterfahrung*, TANZ, 17 (Tübingen: Francke, 1995). See also Hans Werner Günther, *Der Nah- und Enderwartungshorizont in der Apokalypse des heiligen Johannes*, FB, 41 (Würzburg: Echter, 1980).

coming is almost here, only a few years away at the most, empties the proclamation of any meaningful content and robs the message of the *parousia* of its effect. The responsibility of each generation is to work through the key difficult questions rather than being content with 'secondhandedness' if they are to come to a mature faith. Emotion, sentiment, or nostalgia will not do it.[54]

What kind of approach is needed in discussing the question of the delay? In what follows, I shall suggest five basic directions. First of all, it is necessary to get rid of rationalisations and guesswork. The number of unconvincing explanations of the delay in Adventist literature, coming even from scholars, is astonishing. Some of the unsatisfactory answers are based on existential analogies, while others are attempts to find a reference point in ancient culture or to appeal to human logic. For example, it has been suggested that the long interim period between the two advents is to be understood in terms of an existential time or a kind of 'lover's time', which 'is measured not by clock but by love and faith'. According to this idea, the waiting time, regardless of its length, is always perceived as short when experienced in reference to a beloved person. While in the world of love time is real, it 'flies', as in the case of Jacob, of whom it is said that he 'served seven years for Rachel, and they seemed to him but a few days because of the love he had for her' (Gen 29:20).[55] Another creative interpretation appeals to oriental culture, suggesting that in the biblical era the importance of a person could be measured by the length of the delay of his arrival; the more important the person, the longer his delay would be. Since delay indicates importance, according to this suggestion it is natural to expect that the most important wedding ever – the *parousia* – will take place later than expected. While such explanations generally attempt to provide an easy solution, their creativity is not a protection from misguided hopes and expectations.

---

[54] On this, see Bradford, 'Have We Followed a Mirage?'
[55] Bacchiocchi, *Advent Hope*, p. 95.

Secondly, the investigation needs to be rooted in inductive exegetical study of the relevant biblical texts. The analysis needs to give equal weight to two seemingly contradictory strands of thought: imminence and distance statements. While the tension between these two perspectives has caused considerable confusion and given rise to different schools of thought, arriving at its resolution is a hermeneutical challenge necessitating close attention. A balanced path – a *via media* – needs to be trodden to avoid the two false extremes.

Thirdly, the problem of the delay needs to be examined within a salvation-historical scriptural framework. Such an investigation will reveal that the *parousia* is closely tied to the Incarnation-Crucifixion-Resurrection-Ascension Christ event; the two divine acts are 'held apart only by the mercy of God who desires to give men the opportunity for faith and repentance'.[56] In the wider theological context the *parousia* appears as the public, complete fulfilment of the sovereign reign of God inaugurated in the ministry and work of Jesus. It is well known that not only the eschatological day of the Lord, but also the crucifixion and resurrection are seen in terms of apocalyptic and cosmic events (Matt 27:45-53). Therefore, the two mighty acts of God are to be regarded as complementary aspects of his salvific work in Christ.[57] I suggest that examining the problem of delay in the 'already and not yet' eschatological framework of the New Testament

---

[56] C. E. B. Cranfield, *The Gospel According to Mark*, Cambridge Greek Testament (Cambridge: Cambridge University Press, 1963), p. 408.

[57] C. E. B. Cranfield ('St. Mark 13', *SJT*, 6 [1953], 297-305) insists that the events of the Incarnation, Crucifixion, Resurrection and Ascension are 'in a real sense one Event' with the *parousia* (cf. Bacchiocchi, *Advent Hope*, p. 97; Anthony C. Thiselton, *The Last Things: A New Approach* [London: SPCK, 2012], p. 102). It seems, however, that it is more appropriate to speak of two aspects of God's saving act in Christ, manifested in two mighty acts.

has the capacity to resolve the chronological tension, because of the place the New Testament era takes in the biblical storyline.[58]

Fourthly, since God's waiting to conclude the history of this world is part of his response to the problem of evil, understanding the nature of the delay necessitates the examination of its relationship to several key theological issues. The most significant of these are the matters of God's love and his sovereignty and justice, but also the reality of evil, the cosmic conflict and the triumph of God's kingdom. It seems that the problem of the delay is very much like the problem of evil: it is a mystery which cannot be solved in a mechanical way but is to be acknowledged without a demand for a final answer. Still, theological investigation has the capacity to provide some helpful hints and implications, keeping in mind that 'there is no way to ascertain the "cause" (or "causes") of the delay, much less to correct it (or them) in such a manner as to "bring about" the *eschaton*'.[59]

Fifthly, clarifying some essential questions related to the delay is necessary for developing and proclaiming a balanced advent hope. Some of the major questions that deserve clear answers are the following: Is it appropriate to speak of the delay or is the issue a matter of human perception (or misperception)? How shall we relate to the fact of the delay? Can we explain it? Is the time of the Second Coming conditional? What are the nature and the function of the 'signs of the times' and how can they be put into proper perspective? How is it possible to develop a meaningful, balanced expectation of the Second Coming in face of almost 2,000 years of waiting? As is evident, the problem is not only hermeneutical and theological, but also existential.

---

[58] For the significance of this idea for the interpretation of Revelation's language of imminence, see Laszlo Gallusz, 'How Soon is "Soon"? Reading the Language of Eschatological Imminence in the Book of Revelation', in *Faith in Search of Depth and Relevancy. Festschrift in Honour of Dr Bertil Wiklander*, ed. by Reinder Bruinsma (St. Albans: Trans-European Division of Seventh-day Adventists, 2014), pp. 127-45.

[59] Guy, 'Future', p. 228.

5. Conclusion

The sense of delay of the *parousia* is not the result of a divine decision, since God has never set deadlines and changed his mind and postponed them. It is, rather, a human reaction to expectations established by people. Emphasizing the imminence of the Second Coming in an almost time-setting manner will continue to fire a sense of delay and result in disillusionment. I do not suggest that Christ's Second Coming is to be put into some distant future and that we should sit back in false security. In spite of the long waiting time, Adventism needs to live in expectancy, longing for the fulfilment of God's plan for his creation, while at the same time concentrating on serving and witnessing in this world. It should not rely on signs generating false excitement, but follow the insight of Berkouwer, 'The believer is called to an attitude that does not reckon but constantly reckons with the coming of the Lord.'[60] To claim that because Christ's coming is at the door we should be more dedicated in our Christian life is to misunderstand the point. The reality of the cross and the *parousia* should provide sufficient motive for living a certain way of life. While, from a human point of view, our planet has, in the present nuclear age, been brought to the brink of disaster, our approach to the matter of the end and its timing is to recognise that 'God's purposes know no haste and no delay',[61] and that we are still on earth for a reason that only God knows and only he needs to know. For this reason, there is no room for dogmatism in considering the question of delay.

Finally, dare we believe that Jesus is coming soon? Most definitely! While a chronological understanding of 'nearness' is clearly false in light of the waiting period of two thousand years, understanding of the nature of New Testament eschatology helps us to resolve the tension. Whereas Jewish expectations are generally oriented towards a future change or fulfilment, early Christian eschatology is rooted in

---

[60] Berkouwer, *Return*, p. 84.
[61] Ellen White, *Desire of Ages*, p. 32.

the fundamental reference to the victory of a person who has already come, died, been resurrected and has been enthroned. In the light of Easter, the great turning point of salvation history, the time certainly appears short, since the world has entered into the end-time era in which, after Pentecost, the *parousia* is the next major eschatological event to occur in the order of God's redemptive plan and the decisive battle has already been fought and won. In this era the time factor is not a matter of significance (Acts 1: 6-7), since the distance between the two advents is not to be measured chronologically or spatially, but by such concerns as the realisation of God's plan. This perspective frees us from being burdened with the matter of delay or with the direction of current political developments and helps us to appreciate God's plan in which he demonstrates such a degree of loyalty to his created world that he will not take shortcuts that do not work in handling the problem of evil.

'Revival and Reformation'
A Recent Adventist Initiative in a Broader Perspective

Reinder Bruinsma

Introduction

Shortly after Ted N. Wilson was elected in 2010 as the President of the worldwide Seventh-day Adventist Church, he launched a number of initiatives. These were to give direction to the life and ministry of the church in the quinquennium[1] that had started. One of these was named *Revival and Reformation*. Wilson was convinced that the state of the church demanded from the rank and file of the membership a new commitment to the traditional Adventist beliefs and to fervent devotional practices. This paper will review some relevant aspects of calls for revival in the course of church history and the role of aspects of revivalism in early Adventism. It intends to show that this initiative was not as new and unique as many believed it to be. It will, in particular, indicate how many aspects strongly resembled a similar emphasis of the church when Robert H. Pierson was the church's president (1966-1979). It will conclude with some critical remarks and questions and call for in-depth study of a few important elements.

---

[1] Every five years the Seventh-day Adventist Church holds a worldwide congress with delegates from all over the world, to elect leaders and vote plans for the next five-year administrative period.

Revival in the Past

The concept of *Revival and Reformation* is not a recent invention. The emphasis on a special intervention by the Holy Spirit has been a regularly recurring part of the Christian life of faith – from the time of second century Montanism until contemporary Pentecostalism. A long list of persons and movements that emphasised the need for revival could be mentioned. These might include people like Geert Grote (one of the spiritual fathers of the Modern Devotion), John Wycliffe and Jan Hus (precursors of the sixteenth-century Reformation of the Western Church); also Jonathan Edwards, Charles Finney, Billy Sunday and, more recently, Billy Graham – and many more. Seventh-day Adventists, with their roots in the Millerite movement, may arguably be considered as an outgrowth of the Second Great Awakening in America, and thus as having a direct link to a revivalist past.

Yet, if we were to look more closely at the names and movements just mentioned, we would see that the terms 'revival' and 'revivalism' have been applied in a rather broad range of phenomena. The dictionary definitions of 'revival' and 'revivalism' seem straightforward: a *revival* is a re-awakening of religious fervor; or a campaign with meetings, etc. to promote this. *Revivalism* is a state or kind of religion characterised by revival.[2] Gerald L. Priest, a professor of historical religion at the Baptist Theological Seminary in Detroit (USA), however, draws a clear distinction between the term *revival* and the term *revivalism*. He explains how a revival is *God's work* of re-awakening in the individual or in a group of individuals, while he believes revivalism emphasises *the human asp*ect: the methods and techniques used to

---

[2] J Coulson et al., eds, *The Illustrated Oxford Dictionary* (Oxford University Press, 1975 ed.), p. 722. Very similar definitions are given in the *American Heritage Dictionary* (Boston/New York: Houghton Mifflin Company, 1992 ed.).

stimulate a revival.³ Martyn Lloyd-Jones (1899-1981) defined revival as 'an experience in the life of the church when the Holy Spirit does an *unusual* work.'⁴ Richard Lovelace, a popular evangelical author, points us in a somewhat different direction. For him revival primarily denotes *renewal*. It implies an *aggiornamento*, the updating of the church, leading to a new engagement with the surrounding world. Revivals, he says, if understood in the fullest sense, must incorporate spiritual, structural and social transformation.⁵

In exploring what defines revivals, Wesleyan scholar Russell E. Richey, a professor in the Duke Divinity School, lists ten points that are characteristic of revivals. It may be useful to summarize these at the beginning of this paper (as we may recognize many of these points in the specific initiative that is the focus of this study): an underlying pietism, a missional theology, a soteriology of crisis, a jeremiadic understanding of 'these days', the presence of crowds, voluntarism, dramatic ritual form, charismatic leadership, confidence in the Spirit's presence, and a communication network.⁶ Richey also points out that an 'awakening' is a rather sustained series of revivals: '... when a revival becomes contagious and is communicated to the general society; when a revival sustains itself over a prolonged period of time, it becomes an 'awakening'.⁷ Mark Shaw, the director of the World Christianity programme at Africa International University in Nairobi, provides valuable insights into the various dynamics that play a role in revival movements: (1) spiritual factors; (2) cultural factors; (3) historical factors; (4) global, international factors and (5)

---

3   Gerald L. Priest, 'Revival and Revivalism: A Historical and Doctrinal Evaluation', *Detroit Baptist Seminary Journal* 1 (Fall 1996), 223-233.
4   See: http://www.rapidnet.com/~jbeard/bdm/Psychology/revival.htm. Accessed: 2 February 2015.
5   Richard Lovelace, *Dynamics of Spiritual Life* (Downers Grove, IL: InterVarsity Press, 1979), p. 22.
6   Russell E. Richey, 'Revivalism: In Search of a Definition', *Wesleyan Theological Journal* (28, no. 1-2; Spr.-Fall 1993), 171.
7   Richey, ibid., 172.

group dynamics.⁸ Shaw suggests that these five dynamics fit together into one single definition of the revival phenomenon: 'Global revivals are charismatic people movements that seek to transform the world by translating Christian faith and transferring power.'⁹

The *charismatic* element that is common to revivals is not confined to the modern Pentecostal movement that emerged at the beginning of the previous century and has since that time manifested itself in many different forms. Neither has it been limited to the fringe of Protestantism in ages past, nor to the so-called charismatic movement of the 1960s and 1970s,¹⁰ but has been a rather constant constituent of revivals.

The *Second Great Awakening*: Millerism and Early Adventism

The scope of this paper does not allow for a detailed historical, theological, cultural and social analysis of what a revival is and what revivalism stands for. But one point, in particular, has a significant bearing on the Adventist revivalist heritage. American Christianity went through major periods of revival, in particular the First Great Awakening in the eighteenth century, with great men like Jonathan Edwards and George Whitefield, and the Second Great Awakening in the nineteenth century with Charles Finney as the man who towered above all other revivalist preachers.¹¹ To some extent, at least, the

---

[8] Mark Shaw, *Global Awakening: How 20th Century Revivals Triggered a Christian Revelation* (Downers Grove, IL: IVP Academic, 2010), pp. 12-29.
[9] Ibid. 28; see also David Bebbington, *Victorian Religious Revivals: Culture and Piety in Local and Global Contexts* (Oxford: Oxford University Press, 2012), esp. pp. 1-52.
[10] For a succinct description, see Peter Hocken, 'Charismatic Movement', Nicolas Lossky et al., eds., *Dictionary of the Ecumenical Movement* (Geneva: WCC Publications, 1991), pp. 145-149.
[11] For Finney, see Charles E. Hambrick-Stowe, *Charles G. Finney and the Spirit of American Evangelicalism* (Grand Rapids, MI: Eerdmans, 1996).

Millerite movement was part of the Second Great Awakening.[12] It has often been remarked that this Second Awakening – rather than the First Awakening – tended to emphasize the human element in the revival: the techniques and methods that could be followed and would give guaranteed success, whereas the leaders of the First Awakening tended to regard revivals primarily as the 'surprising work' of God. Moreover, the First Awakening was much more concerned with doctrinal purity than the revival wave that went over America in the nineteenth century.[13]

The Second Awakening is usually dated from about 1790 to about 1840. This period of revivalism, historian William G. McLoughlin (1922-1992) explains, not only spawned a great number of sects and nourished a large number of established denominations, but it also influenced most of America's social reforms of that era.[14] He underlines the close relationship between the revivalism of the Second Great Awakening and the emergence of millennialism and Adventism,[15] both in its Millerite and later phases. William Miller (1782-1849) understood himself as a 'non-sectarian' – that is, not as a preacher of the doctrines of one specific denomination, but rather as a tool in God's hand to 'revive' people in all different 'sects' (denominations)

[12] There is an abundance of literature on these two movements. See e.g. William G. McLoughlin, *Revivals, Awakening and Reform: An Essay on Religion and Social Change in America, 1607-1977* (Chicago and London: University of Chicago Press, 1978), esp. pp. 45-140; Mark A. Knoll, *A History of Christianity in the United States and Canada* (Grand Rapids, MI: Eerdmans, 1992),pp. 85-113; 165-190; Sydney E. Ahlstrom, *A Religious History of the American People* (New Haven and London: Yale University Press, 1972), pp. 280-313; 415-454; Martin E. Marty, *Pilgrims in Their Own Land: 500 Years of Religion in America* (New York: Penguin, 1984), pp. 108-126; 169-176.
[13] For a clear description of the differences in nature between the First and the Second Great Awakening, see Gerald L. Priest, ibid., pp. 229-250.
[14] William G. Mcloughlin. 'Revivalism', in Edwin Scott Gaustad, ed., *The Rise of Adventism* (New York: Harper & Row, 1974), pp. 119-151.
[15] Ibid., p. 120.

and to alert them to the fact that they lived at the end of time.¹⁶ In a recent book on William Miller and the Millerite movement¹⁷ Adventist church historian George Knight agrees with this position and that of several other scholars: Millerism is to be regarded as the final segment of the Second Great Awakening.¹⁸ He states: 'The rise of Adventism took place during America's greatest religious revival.... Millerism was born into a world excited with religion and religious themes. Religion was a dynamic, growing enterprise in the United States, and Millerism was well adapted to capitalize on the dynamic expansion.'¹⁹

Charles Finney (1793-1875) has often been described as the master-revivalist of the nineteenth century. Although Miller and Finney were contemporaries, it appears that they never actually met, even though there were some indirect contacts. Finney, at one time, tried to convince Miller that his premillennialist view was faulty.²⁰ Miller and other early Millerite and post-Millerite Adventist leaders were, no doubt, aware of Finney's theology in general as well as of his pragmatic approach to revivalism. Finney's 'new measures', such as the 'anxious bench' and the 'protracted meetings', were fiercely debated and remained controversial.²¹ His book *Lectures on Revivals in Religion* (1835) was a kind of manual on how to conduct a revival and stressed the human elements in bringing about a revival.²²

---

[16] David T. Arthur, 'Millerism,' in Edwin Scott Gaustad, ed., *The Rise of Adventism* (New York: Harper & Row, 1974), pp. 154, 155.
[17] To a large extent based on his earlier work: George R. Knight, *Millennial Fever and the End of the World* (Boise, ID: Pacific Press, 1993).
[18] George R. Knight, *William Miller and the Rise of Adventism* (Boise, ID: Pacific Press, 2010), p. 19.
[19] Ibid., 8.
[20] Knight, *Millennial Fever*, p. 139.
[21] Charles F. Hambrick-Stowe, 'Charles G. Finney', in Mark G. Toulouse and James O. Duke, eds., *Makers of Christian Theology in America* (Nashville, TN: Abingdon Press, 1997), pp. 130-134.
[22] Derek J. Tidball, *Who are the Evangelicals? Tracing the Roots of Today's Movements* (London: Marshall Pickering, 1994), pp. 59-60.

An aspect that ought to be mentioned is the large Methodist influence on the period in general and on the Millerite movement and the later Seventh-day Adventist movement in particular. Several later leaders, among them Ellen G. White (1827-1915), had a Methodist background. The revivalist fervour of early Methodism is well known,[23] as is the relationship between Methodism and the later holiness movement.[24]

Nineteenth century revivals were closely linked with *Reform* movements,[25] in particular campaigns protesting alcohol and slavery.[26] Several Millerite leaders and early post-Millerite Adventist leaders were active in social reforms. Ellen White was one of them. Not only did she champion health reform and temperance, but she also advocated dress reform and religious liberty.[27] In this respect she and others definitely stood in the tradition of nineteenth century revivalism.[28] 'All reformers, including non-evangelicals and ones who left their churches, owed much to revivalism.'[29]

---

[23] Richard P. Heizenrater, *Wesley and the People Called Methodists* (Nashville, TN: Abingdon Press, 1995), in particular pp. 97-146; see also Howard A. Snyder, 'John Wesley Redfield: a study in nineteenth century American Methodist revivalism,' in *Wesleyan Theological Journal* (41, no 1: Spr. 2006), 205-222; and Ann Tavis, 'Visions', Terrie Dopp Aamodt et al., eds., *Ellen Harmon White: American Prophet* (Oxford, New York: Oxford University Press, 2014), pp. 33-38.

[24] For a short description, see Ahlstrom, *A Religious History*, pp. 816-819.

[25] A classic on this topic is: Timothy L. Smith, *Revivalism and Social Reform in Mid-Nineteenth-Century America* (New York, Nashville TN: Abingdon Press, 1957).

[26] Ahlstrom, pp. 640-669.

[27] Douglas Morgan, 'Society', in *Ellen Harmon White: American Prophet, pp. 224-243.*

[28] See Ronald G. Walters, *American Reformers 1815-1860* (New York: Hill and Wang, 1978).

[29] Walters, ibid., p. 37.

A Few Relevant Aspects of Seventh-day Adventist History

Seventh-day Adventism has never tried to distance itself from its revivalist roots in the Second Great Awakening. But although terms like 'revival' and 'reformation' retained a positive connotation in Adventism, from the very beginning it consistently denounced (what was called) 'charismatic' extremes and stressed the possibility and danger of 'false' revivals. Most Adventist believers recognized the gift of prophecy, as exercised by Ellen White, as a true sign of the presence of the Holy Spirit in their midst and were also prepared to seek for, and accept, forms of the gift of healing. However, other 'gifts', such as glossolalia and various physically deviant behaviors, were soon labelled as fanaticism and extremism, and the threat of 'mesmerism' and similar phenomena was always kept in mind.[30]

To what extent 'extreme' charismatic elements were present in the earliest years of the Adventist Church is difficult to determine.[31] They have often been downplayed by later church representatives, but recent research has discovered examples that were mostly unknown – at least to the general church membership.[32] A case that in recent years has kindled considerable interest was that of Israel Damman (also spelled as Damon or Dammon). It has been suggested that the evidence indicates that Ellen White (in 1845) was personally involved in some strange ecstatic actions – or at least present when these occurred.[33] In the early 1970s Arthur L. White, a grandson of Ellen White, wrote twelve articles for the Adventist denominational

---

[30] For the relationship between revivalism and mesmerism, see e.g. Brett E. Carroll, *Spiritualism in Antebellum America* (Bloomington & Indianapolis: Indiana University Press, 1997), pp. 112, 113.

[31] Richard W. Schwartz and Floyd Greenleaf, *Light Bearers: A History of the Seventh-day Adventist Church* (Boise, ID: Pacific Press, 2000 ed.), p. 54.

[32] Michael W. Campbell, 'Ecstatic Experiences', in Denis Fortin and Jerry Moon, eds., *The Ellen White Encyclopedia* (Hagerstown, MD: Review and Herald, 2013), pp. 791-793.

[33] James R. Nix, 'Damman', *The Ellen White Encyclopedia*, 358-360; Rennie Schoeplin, ed. 'Scandal or Rite of Passage? Historians on the Dammon Trial', *Spectrum*, 18:2 (1987), 37-50.

journal *Review and Herald* about *'Charismatic Experiences in Early Adventist History'* in which some specific cases are mentioned.³⁴ By way of introduction Arthur White quotes a 1850 statement from his grandmother that summarizes what she continued to underline: 'I saw that we should strive at all times to be free from unhealthy and unnecessary excitement.'³⁵ This consistently remained her position and the view of the Seventh-day Adventist Church. From the early twentieth century onwards, the fear of charismatic fanaticism was, however, probably not just inspired by memories of the past, but also by worries that modern Pentecostalism might make its inroads into Adventism.

Occasionally, however, charismatic excesses did occur in Adventism. One of the best-known examples was the 'Holy Flesh' movement in Indiana around 1899-1900. The movement had its roots in a holiness thrust that began sweeping through Adventism in North America in 1892. A more radical form erupted a few years later when a considerable group of people – among them A.F. Ballenger (1861-1921; known mostly because his opposition against the traditional Adventist sanctuary doctrine) – came to believe that the outpouring of the Holy Spirit, promised as 'the latter rain', was about to occur.³⁶ The baptism of the Holy Spirit would bring victory over all sin and even over all sickness – much in line with contemporary holiness preaching in other denominations. Some, however, took this much further and claimed that true conversion would result in a 'translation' of earthly flesh into incorruptible flesh.³⁷

---

[34] *Review and Herald*, 10, 17, 24 August 1972; 15, 22, 29 March 1973; 5, 12, 19, 26 April 1973; 2, 9 August 1973.
[35] The statement is found in Ellen G. White, *Manuscript* 11, 1850.
[36] *Light Bearers*, 615, 616; Lowell Tarling, *The Edges of Seventh-day Adventism: A Study of Separatist Groups Emerging from the Seventh-day Adventist Church (1844-1980)* (Bermagui South, 1981), pp. 84-83; Calvin W. Edwards and Gary Land, *Seeker after Light: A.F. Ballenger. Adventism and American Christianity* (Berrien Springs, MI: Andrews University Press, 2000), pp. 36-53.
[37] Gary Land, 'Holy Flesh', in *The Ellen G. White Encyclopedia*, pp. 873-874.

Through the years there have been periodic reports of revivals in local Adventist churches. There has, in particular, been a considerable amount of preaching on topics as the 'former' and 'latter rain' and related eschatological events. In recent decades the need to develop one's spiritual gifts has been stressed by some[38] and a few books have been written about the person and work of the Holy Spirit[39] and about the gift of tongues.[40]

Ellen G. White has written about 'revival and reformation', but not as much as many might think. In fact, an electronic search of her books only produces about 200 hits, and many of these are found closely together in a limited number of passages, in just a few publications. Moreover, in many places two particular statements are often repeated. In 1887 she wrote an article entitled 'The Church's Need' which contains the well-known statement: 'A revival of true godliness among us is the greatest and most urgent of all our needs.'[41] She continues in the article:

> The church must arouse to action. The Spirit of God can never come in until she prepares the way. There should be earnest searching of heart. There should be united, persevering prayer, and through faith a claiming of the promises of God. There should be, not a clothing of the body with sackcloth, as in ancient times, but a deep humiliation of soul. We have not the

---
[38] See e.g. http://women.adventistconnect.org/spiritual-gifts-inventory; accessed 3 February 2015.
[39] E.g. Leroy E. Froom, *The Coming of the Comforter* (Washington, DC: Review and Herald, 1931); Morris L. Venden, *Your Friend the Holy Spirit* (Boise, ID: Pacific Press, 1986); Jan Paulsen, *When the Spirit Descends* (Hagerstown, MD: Review and Herald, 2001 ed.).
[40] Roland R. Hegstad, *Rattling the Gates* (Washington DC: Review and Herald, 1974); Gerhard F. Hasel, *Speaking in Tongues: Biblical Speaking in Tongues and Contemporary Glossolalia* (Berrien Springs, MI: Adventist Theological Society Publications, 1991); William E. Richardson, *Speaking in Tongues* (Hagerstown, MD: Review and Herald, 1994).
[41] Ellen G. White, 'The Church's Need', *Review and Herald*, 22 March 1887.

first reason for self-congratulation and self-exaltation. We should humble ourselves under the mighty hand of God. He will appear to comfort and bless the true seekers.

In a second, also often cited, article, written some fifteen years later, Mrs. White links the concept of 'reformation' with the concept of 'revival':

> A revival and a reformation must take place, under the ministration of the Holy Spirit. Revival and reformation are two different things. Revival signifies a renewal of spiritual life, a quickening of the powers of mind and heart, a resurrection from spiritual death. Reformation signifies a reorganization, a change in ideas and theories, habits and practices. Reformation will not bring forth the good fruit of righteousness unless it is connected with revival of the Spirit. Revival and reformation are to do their appointed work, and in doing this work they must blend.[42]

We will see these quotes returning over and over again, in particular during the General Conference presidencies of Robert H. Pierson and Ted N. C. Wilson. Although other church leaders – general conference presidents among them – have spoken, preached and written about the need for revival and reformation – albeit in a modified form, without the 'excitement' of the revival atmosphere that early Adventism inherited – .the theme only emerged in full force in the Robert Pierson (1911-1989) era, as he led the Adventist denomination from 1966 until 1979.

---

[42] Ellen White, 'The Need of a Revival and a Reformation', *Review and Herald*, 25 February 1902.

Robert Pierson as Champion of Revival and Reformation

Pierson was very concerned about the nearly two decades of alleged 'liberalizing' tendencies under President Reuben H. Figuhr, and was determined to steer the church in another direction. Raymond Cottrell (1911-2003), a prominent editor of the Review and Herald and of the seven-volume SDA Bible Commentary, described Pierson in these words: 'Robert H. Pierson was a gracious person, a dedicated Adventist, a gentleman in every way, but also a person with clear objectives and resolute determination to achieve them.' He saw 'Pierson, Gordon M. Hyde and Gerhard Hasel (1935-1994) as the three architects behind 'the decade of obscurantism (1969-1979)'. According to Cottrell this 'triumvirate' attempted to gain control of Adventist biblical studies in this decade.[43]

During the Annual Council (then named the Fall Council) of 1973 the Pierson administration launched a 'revival and reformation' initiative. Pierson proposed nine areas of special focus, as the church would concentrate on 'revival and reformation'.

1. An unprepared church.

2. The message being subtly attacked through questioning the inspiration of the Bible and the Spirit of Prophecy.

3. Institutions that need redirection by their board chairman and administration.

4. Church leadership in need of revival and recommitment.

5. A church drifting away from the study of God's Word – a need for revival in Bible study.

6. Homes that need help to cope with modern pressures – a need to establish the 'family altar'.

7. Need for 'first-love' witnessing.

---

[43] http://en.wikipedia.org/wiki/Raymond_Cottrell, accessed February 2015.

8. Need for 'first-love' giving.
9. Need for a revival of Bible-based preaching that stresses Christ our righteousness.[44]

Pierson's book *Revival and Reformation*,[45] and his emotional farewell speech in 1973, after he resigned from the presidency for health reasons, expressed to a large extent the same concerns – as illustrated in the following quote:

> Regrettably, there are those in the church who belittle the inspiration of the total Bible, who scorn the first 11 chapters of Genesis, who question the Spirit of Prophecy's short chronology of the age of the earth, and who subtly and not so subtly attack the Spirit of Prophecy. There are some who point to the reformers and contemporary theologians as a source and the norm for Seventh-day Adventist doctrine. There are those who allegedly are tired of the hackneyed phrases of Adventism. There are those who wish to forget the standards of the church we love. There are those who covet and would court the favor of the evangelicals; those who would throw off the mantle of a peculiar people; and those who would go the way of the secular, materialistic world.
>
> Fellow leaders, beloved brethren and sisters – don't let it happen! I appeal to you as earnestly as I know how this morning – don't let it happen! I appeal to Andrews University, to the Seminary, to Loma Linda University – don't let it happen! We are not Seventh-day Anglicans, not Seventh-day Lutherans – we are

---

[44] *Minutes General Conference Committee*, 15 October 1973. http://documents.adventistarchives.org/Minutes/GCC/GCC1973-10a.pdf
[45] Robert H. Pierson, *Revival and Reformation* (Washington, DC: Review and Herald, 1974).

Seventh-day Adventists! This is God's last church with God's last message![46]

One cannot to fail to notice the great similarity between the 'revival and reformation' emphasis of Robert Pierson and that of Ted N. C. Wilson, a few decades later, as David J. B. Trim, the director of the denomination's archives, also pointed out in a recent *Adventist Review* article.[47]

The Theme of Revival in the 1980-2010 Period

During the presidency of Neal C. Wilson (1979-1990; the father of Ted N. C. Wilson) 'revival and reformation' was not a major theme. It returned during the presidency of Robert F. Folkenberg (1990-1999), although his preferred term was 'total commitment.' A document entitled *Total Commitment* was approved by the church's Annual Council held in 1996 in Costa Rica.[48] Folkenberg's attempt to have all leaders and senior teachers in the church sign a document in which they would pledge their 'total commitment' – in particular to Adventist traditional doctrine – was highly controversial, to say the least, and was never implemented in the way he envisaged.[49] A modified *Total Commitment* document found its way, however, into the *Policy Book* of the world church.[50]

---

[46] Robert H. Pierson, 'Final Appeal to God's People', *Review and Herald*, 26 October 1973.

[47] David J. B. Trim, 'Revival and Reformation Revisited: Lessons from the 1973 Annual Conference', *Adventist Review*, Special Feature: http://www.adventistreview.org/141528-20

[48] R. Dabrowski, ed., 'Total Commitment to God', in *Statements, Guidelines and Other Documents, Seventh-day Adventist Church* (Silver Spring, MD: General Conf. Of SDA, Communication Dept., 2005), p. 237.

[49] I was a church administrator at the time and a member of the GC Committee and am therefore well acquainted with these developments. I remember also lively discussions about this among the staff at Newbold College.

[50] *SDA Working Policy*, Policy A 15.

For Jan Paulsen (GC president 1999-2010), the main challenge was the unity of the church, in spite of all its rich diversity. As referred to above, he wrote a book on the person and work of the Holy Spirit.[51] Glancing through the titles of the many articles he wrote for church publications, it is clear that he also saw the need for revival and reformation and for complete commitment, but his primary emphasis was on the unity of the church and on the moral responsibilities of the church and its members in society.[52]

Ted N. C. Wilson and the *Revival and Reformation* Initiative

As soon as Ted N. C. Wilson had been elected General Conference president, he expressed his main burdens for the church in his significant sermon in Atlanta on July 3, 2010. The title of his sermon *Go Forward* may well have been inspired by the 'Go Forward' message in the last volume of Ellen White's *Testimonies*.[53] This going forward was to be manifested in a number of different areas that since 'Atlanta' have become the staple of Wilson's messages at major meetings:

- do not reach out to megachurches and movements outside of Adventism.

- do not 'succumb to fanatical or loose theology that wrestles God's Word from the pillars of biblical truth and the landmark beliefs of the Seventh-day Adventist Church'; stay with a 'plain reading' of the Bible.

---

[51] Cf. Note 36.
[52] For a complete bibliography of Paulsen's publications, see 'Jan Paulsen: Select Bibliography' in Borge Schantz and Reinder Bruinsma, eds., *Exploring the Frontiers of Faith: Festschrift in Honor of Dr Jan Paulsen* (Lueneburg, Germany: Advent Verlag, 2009), pp. 17-28.
[53] Ellen G. White, *Testimonies for the Church*, vol. 9 (Mountain View, CA: Pacific Press, 1948 ed.). p. 271.

- do not misinterpret the first eleven chapters of Genesis or other areas of Scripture as allegorical or merely symbolic; God created the world in 'six literal, consecutive, contiguous 24 hour days;' do not accept any form of theistic evolution.
- stay far away from the historical-critical methods of explaining the Bible.
- the Spirit of Prophecy is 'be read, believed, applied and promoted.'

At the end of the sermon Wilson asked the 70,000-strong audience to 'plead with the Lord for revival and reformation, so that the Holy Spirit can lead God's remnant church.'[54]

A detailed appeal for revival in the church came during the Annual Council of the same year (2010), when a document entitled 'God's Promised Gift' was voted.[55] It focused on the divine promise of the 'latter rain', and quoted the key Ellen G. White statements about revival and reformation, including her statement about the difference between revival and reformation:

> A revival and a reformation ... are two different things. Revival signifies renewal of spiritual life, a quickening of the powers of the mind and heart, a resurrection from spiritual death. Reformation signifies a reorganization, a change in ideas and theories, habits and practices. Reformation will not bring forth the good fruit of righteousness unless it is connected with reformation of the Spirit. Revival and reformation are

---

[54] For a transcript of this sermon, see *Adventist Review, GC Session Bulletin no. 8.*, 9 July 2010.
[55] 'God's Promised Gift', Annual Council action, 10 November 2010. For the text, see http://www.revivalandreformation.org/uploaded_assets/41921 The text was also printed in various church media, as e.g. *Ministry* magazine. See: https://www.ministrymagazine.org/archive/2010/12/gods-promised-gift

to do to do their appointed work, and in doing this work they must blend.⁵⁶

The document emphasized the need for the special outpouring of the Holy Spirit, symbolized by the 'latter rain'. The revival that is wanted is the 'last mighty revival' that is to take place on earth. An earnest appeal was made to form a global circle of prayer at 7:00 o'clock every morning and to have a worldwide emphasis on the reading of the God's Word. The purpose of this outpouring of the Spirit 'in latter rain power' is to finish Christ's mission on earth so He can come quickly.

Just a few weeks later, Wilson preached to a *Generation of Youth for Christ* meeting in Baltimore. Wilson's unreserved endorsement of this youth organisation that runs parallel to the church's official youth work, and is in many ways very critical of it, caused considerable discussion. The participants found on their seats a copy of a 96-page compilation of Ellen G. White statements about 'true revival'⁵⁷ and the theme of individual and collective revival was a major element of this sermon.⁵⁸

The *Revival and Reformation* initiative was soon strengthened by a number of administrative measures. A committee was established at the General Conference level, and a vice-president (Armando Miranda) was given special oversight of this initiative. The committee was first named *Revival and Reformation* committee and was later renamed the *Revival and Beyond* committee.⁵⁹ Subsidiary initiatives were developed, such as a special website,⁶⁰ and facilities to assist

---

⁵⁶ Ellen. G. White, *Selected Messages*, vol. 1, p. 128.
⁵⁷ Very soon after Wilson's election this book was compiled and published by the Review and Herald Publishing Association: *True Revival: The Church's Greatest Need* (2010).
⁵⁸ For the text of the sermon, see http://perspectives.adventist.org/sermons/sermons/go/2011-01-01/generation-of-youth-for-christ/6/
⁵⁹ See Adventist News Network Report: http://news.adventist.org/en/all-news/news/go/2010-09-28/spirituality-committee-proffering-ideas-for-revival/
⁶⁰ http://www.revivalandreformation.org/

the church members in bringing their Bible reading habits and their prayer life to a different level, such as the *Revived by His Word* plan[61] and the *777 Prayer Chain*.[62]

The Annual Council meetings in the 2010-2015 quinquennium were the occasions *par excellence* for the General Conference president to lay before the church his concerns and ideals. The sermons by Wilson on those occasions in 2011, 2012, 2013 and 2014 give us a further insight into his convictions as to how a global revival and reformation in the church is to be realized.[63] The main elements keep repeating themselves: Faithfulness to the Bible and a 'plain reading' of the biblical text, faithfulness to the Spirit of Prophecy, and a mission outreach based on traditional concepts. Many of the same aspects are also highlighted in Wilson's 2012 book: *Almost Home: A Call to Revival and Reformation* – a book with, admittedly, a remarkably mild tone.[64] A special emphasis on belief in a six-day literal creation featured high in Wilson's keynote address at the International Bible and Science Conference in Las Vegas, Nevada in August 2014. There he went as far as to say: 'If one does not accept the recent six-day creation understanding then that person is actually not a "Seventh-day Adventist."'[65] It has been noted that Wilson has made similar

---

[61] http://revivedbyhisword.org/
[62] http://www.revivalandreformation.org/777
[63] The transcripts of the sermons have been printed in the *Adventist Review*: 2011: 'Mission to the Cities – Comprehensive Urban Evangelism', *Adventist Review*, 24 October 2013; 2012: 'Never Doubt – God is in Control,' *Adventist Review*, 13 October 2012; 'Communicate God's Truth in Love and Illuminate the Earth with God's Glory', *Adventist Review*, 12 October 2013: 'God's Prophetic Movement, Message, and Mission and their Attempted Neutralization by the Devil', *Adventist News*, 11 October 2014.
[64] Published by Pacific Press Publishing Association (Nampa, ID), 2012.
[65] For a transcript of the address, see http://perspectives.adventist.org/sermons/sermons/go/2014-08-15/gods-authoritative-voice/.

statements with regard to people who, in his view, deviate from normative Adventism in other doctrinal areas.[66]

Some Critical Remarks

Revivals have not always been welcomed by Christian churches and Christian leaders,[67] and some revivalist approaches have come under intense criticism.[68] In today's Seventh-day Adventism the *Revival and Reformation* initiative, and many aspects that are associated with it, have led to considerable discussion and polarisation. This study, that, admittedly, has been far from exhaustive, leaves us with a number of issues that invite further study.

1. More historical awareness of church history in general, on the part of key Adventist leaders, would enable them to place the current Adventist 'revival and reformation' in a broader historical perspective, with a clearer understanding of the various ways in which revival terminology has been used. It might be wise to reconsider the use of some of this terminology.

2. The kind of revival advocated by Pierson and Wilson is not so much a traditional 'revival', focused on the 'saving of unconverted souls' by preaching the basics of the gospel, but rather a revitalisation of the saints with an emphasis on doctrinal purity. Traditional Adventist evangelism in a third world or immigrant context may actually have more in common with the kind of revivals of the First Great

---

[66] E.g. Lawrence Downing, 'An Open Letter to My Pastoral and Academic Colleagues', 31 August 2014 on the Adventist Today website: http://atoday.org/open-letter-pastoral-academic-colleagues-2.html

[67] See e.g. "Revival in the Church. Do We Need It? Is It Biblical?' http://www.rapidnet.com/~jbeard/bdm/Psychology/revival.htm; 'The Dangers of Revivals and of their Critics', http://oldlife.org/2011/07/the-danger-of-revivals-and-of-their-critics/

[68] Mark A. Noll, *A History of Christianity*, pp. 175-176.

Awakening and the Second Great Awakening than with the revival Pierson and Wilson envisaged.

3. Placing the current 'revival and reformation' initiative against the background of a broader Adventist history may give a more balanced and somewhat relativized perspective of what to expect from this initiative. Wilson's initiative may be compared with that of Robert Pierson and is far from unique. Church history and Adventist history tend to confirm the theory that revivals occur (or are sought) in periodic waves.[69]

4. In post-Reformation times *reformation* has usually (and certainly in the USA) been understood as predominantly social in nature. President Jan Paulsen may have understood this better that either Pierson or Wilson, who are especially interested in a renewed focus on hermeneutics and doctrinal aspects. It would be more in line with Adventist tradition to (also) stress social responsibilities and reforms.

5. Revivals have usually been characterized by a desire to include as many people as possible in the experience of salvation. The current *revival and reformation* initiative has a significant tendency to be exclusive rather than to be inclusive: Those who do not uphold certain doctrinal standards show hereby that they are not 'genuine' Adventists. The eschatological concept of the 'shaking' (the falling-away of unfaithful believers in the time of the end) is also regularly linked to the 'revival.'

6. There is much emphasis on the presence of the Spirit, and especially on the theme of the 'latter rain', and on the continued threat of 'false' manifestations of the Spirit, while there is very little theological attention to the doctrine of the Holy Spirit and the theology of the spiritual gifts. One may

---

[69] Michael Barkun, 'The Awakening-Cycle Controversy', *SA Sociological Analysis* (46 no. 4; winter 1985), 425-443.

wonder whether this is not a strange omission when 'revival' is such a prominent topic.

7. The administrative and organisational measures to promote the current *'revival and reformation'* initiative beg the question whether perhaps too much is being orchestrated (cf. Finney's 'new measures'), and too little left to the initiative of the Spirit himself. This latter aspect is underlined by this striking quote from a British theologian:

> The failure to distinguish between divine and human activity leads to a distorted view of the Church. The preservation of the community's identity becomes too vital a task, since it identifies itself and its goals too closely with God and his purposes. Thus, what the community and its leaders want is what God wants. So, the task of the community moves from an open engagement in social interrelationships quickened by the Spirit (mission) to being a closed agenda, in which God and the community only confront the world in a defensive fashion . . .'[70]

Conclusions

At the time of the writing of this paper some five years have passed since the launching of the *Revival and Reformation* initiative that was very much linked to President Ted Wilson's personal burden for this perceived need. When Wilson was re-elected as the church's president in the summer of 2015, the theme was once again emphasized as one of the needs of the denomination, but a more pragmatic and action-oriented initiative (*Total Member Involvement*) was pushed to the number one slot for the next five years. Was the emphasis on Revival

---

[70] Martyn Percy, *Words, Wonders and Power: Understanding Contemporary Christian Fundamentalism and Revivalism* (London: SPCK, 1996), p. 27.

and Reformation no longer needed to the same extent as it was five years earlier? Or had it simply run out of steam?

At least two aspects of the *Revival and Reformation* initiative require urgent further in-depth study:

1. It is of course, very difficult to quantify the results of something like the *Revival and Reformation* initiative. Yet it is important to get a much clearer idea than we currently have about the impact of the various elements this 'campaign'. Did it influence a significant number of people towards a deeper religious commitment, as would, for instance, be visible in their devotional habits? If there was a definite impact, was this only positive? Or did the related emphasis on doctrinal purity tend to increase polarisation in the church?

2. It seems clear that the Adventist Church must acquire a deeper theological and historical understanding of what 'revival' and 'reformation' mean. Some critical issues must be addressed, in particular: What role, if any, have church administrators/leaders in the origin, strengthening and 'management' of revivals and reformations? And to what extent is doctrinal purity a key element in true revival?

Answers to these and related questions will help the Adventist Church to learn from past experiences and perhaps help to relate adequately to future calls for revival and reformation.

Fundamental Beliefs; Curse or Blessing?

On the Pros and Cons of Adventist Confessional Statements

Rolf J Pöhler

From their beginnings in the late 1840s until today, Seventh-day Adventists have denied the need for a creed, believing it would hamper the continuous exploration of the Scriptures in search of 'present truth'. In recent decades, however, the so-called 'Fundamental Beliefs' have gradually assumed the function of a creedal statement used in defining the boundaries of the Adventist faith for converts and members alike. This is a noticeable departure from the traditional Adventist view. What are the reasons for this development? Where will it lead to? What is the role and value of a statement of faith? Is it needed at all if the Bible itself is regarded as 'the only rule of faith and practice'? How do Adventists deal with the tension between the exclusivity and sufficiency of the Scriptures and the binding character of their 28 points of faith?

In view of the 2015 General Conference Session in San Antonio, this issue is highly relevant and controversial for Adventists in general and theologians in particular. How will the changes in the Fundamental Beliefs statement affect the church? How are they to be evaluated in the light of Scripture, Christian and Adventist history, and the contemporary world? Is such a statement actually beneficial and useful, or unnecessary and even harmful? Are the Fundamental Beliefs essential in their present form or should they be replaced by a more concise statement of faith? This paper explores these and related questions, analyzing the current situation, evaluating trends, and exploring possible alternatives. What role can and should Fundamental Beliefs play in the life and faith of the church? Do they foster, or hinder, the ongoing need for reformation in the church (ecclesia reformata semper reformanda)?

Part 1
Why the Church Does (not) Need a 'Creed'

Do Seventh-day Adventists Have a Creed?

One of the oldest Christian confessions simply says: 'I believe that Jesus Christ is the Son of God.' (Acts 8:37)[1] The shortest statements of the Christian faith consist of just two words: 'Jesus (is the) Christ', and 'Christ (is the) Lord.' (Cf. John 20:28; Acts 2:36) What the first Christians expressed in a few words or in a single sentence was later elaborated and replaced by detailed statements that expressed the principal teachings of the Christian church and churches. Thus, 'creeds' (from the Latin *credo*, I believe) became the common foundation of Christian faith and teaching. They are still regarded as foundational to the Christian church and recited week by week in

---

[1] While this verse is not found in the oldest Greek manuscripts, it seems to reflect an ancient Christian practice. All Scripture references are taken from the NRSV.

worship services around the world.² During the time of the Protestant Reformation, a number of new Confessions were written up, which expressed and professed the biblically grounded teachings of the Anglican, Lutheran, and Reformed churches. In them, Protestants took pains to explain and defend their disagreement with some of the traditional doctrines of the Roman Catholic Church.

Likewise, Seventh-day Adventists have expressed their basic teachings in the form of brief articles of faith geared toward the general public. They thereby wanted to live up to the exhortation of the apostle Peter who admonished Christians of his time: 'Always be ready to make your defense to anyone who demands from you an accounting for the hope that is in you.' (1 Pet 3:15) Still, Adventists do not claim to have a 'creed' or 'confession of faith'; instead, they speak of 'Fundamental Beliefs' or 'points of faith'. By these are meant those articles of faith that summarise the main teachings of the Adventist church. Whether, or to what extent, this distinction is of importance remains to be seen.

Historical Position Toward Church Confessions

What characterised early Sabbath-keeping Adventists was their strong and united rejection of any creed having binding authority on believers. In their view, 'The Bible, and the Bible alone, is to be our creed, the sole bond of union.'³ Repeatedly, the 'pioneers' of the church – first and foremost James and Ellen White – emphasised the

---

[2] For a comprehensive listing of Christian creeds, see *Creeds of the Churches: A Reader in Christian Doctrine from the Bible to the Present*, rev. ed., ed. by John H. Leith (Atlanta, AL; John Knox Press, 1963/1973). Seventh-day Adventists have expressed their basic approval and support of the so-called 'Apostles' Creed', though it is not recited in Adventist worship services. See W. R. Beach, *The Creed That Changed the World* (Mountain View, CA: Pacific Press, 1971); this book appeared in the wake of Vatican Council II in which Adventists participated as observers.

[3] Ellen G. White, *Selected Messages*, vol. 1 (Washington, DC: Review & Herald, 1958), p. 416.

unique role of the Scriptures as 'the only rule of faith and practice'.[4] Nothing should hamper the progressive understanding of the Word of God, no compulsory church confession should hinder believers from discovering truth for themselves and following the dictates of their own conscience. In this estimation, Sabbatarian Adventists were not alone. Many of them had come from, or were influenced by, the so-called 'Restoration Movement', which wanted to overcome the divisions of Christianity by returning to the 'primitive' (original) faith as set forth in the New Testament, uniting believers on the plain teachings of the Bible as the norm of all Christian faith and practice. The slogan 'No creed but the Bible!' was expressive of this view.[5]

In the light of Christian history, where often enough an oppressive church had forced its dogmas on believers, denying their right to study the Bible for themselves and to follow their own insights, early Adventists saw in church creeds an instrument of control by which the church exerted her abusive power. To them creeds were an unmistakable sign of Babylonian confusion and apostasy – Catholic and Protestant alike (Rev 12-18). When, in the early 1860s, James White began to organise the Sabbatarian movement into a Christian denomination, there was widespread fear that – in spite of the best of intentions – such a move would lead to the establishment of another church that one day would become intolerant and oppressive as others had been before. This fear of a gradual relapse into Babylonian structures was most forcefully expressed by John Loughborough in 1861:

> The *first* step of apostasy is to get up a creed, telling us what we shall believe. The *second* is, to make that creed

---

[4] *A Word to the 'Little Flock'* (Brunswick, ME: James White, 1847), 13. For more such quotations, see Rolf J. Pöhler, 'Adventisten, Ellen White und das Sola-Scriptura-Prinzip', *Spes Christiana* 17 (2006):45-48 (45-68).

[5] On Christian Restorationism in nineteenth century North America and its impact on Adventism, see Rolf J. Pöhler, *Continuity and Change in Adventist Teaching*, Friedensauer Schriftenreihe A. Theologie, Bd. 3 (Frankfurt: Peter Lang, 2000), 27-30.

a test of fellowship. The *third* is to try members by that creed. The *fourth* [is] to denounce as heretics those who do not believe that creed. And, *fifth*, to commence persecution against such.[6]

When, in 1883, the adoption of a Church Manual containing 'simple rules' and 'suggestions only' was proposed, it was opposed by a majority of the delegates of the General Conference as being unnecessary and potentially dangerous. A major reason for its rejection was the fear of a growing uniformity and a gradual fixing of the Adventist faith.[7] However, only two years later the mood was beginning to change as doctrinal controversies arose, causing some to look for other means than the Bible of keeping the church united in faith.

Changing Attitudes Toward Creedal Statements[8]

Since the mid-1880s, new and conflicting views on exegetical and doctrinal matters had been troubling the church. They involved the function of the law in the process of salvation and the interpretation of apocalyptic symbols (10 horns, Dan 7). To counter such divergent views, ministers were expected to adhere to all the fundamental doctrines of the church. Several articles in the *Review & Herald* argued that some kind of creed was necessary in order to prevent errors from creeping into the church and to teach the true faith. While the term creed was freely used, it was not understood in the sense of a fixed rule of faith. It was also emphasised that the Bible remained the ultimate source of appeal.[9]

---

6 'Doings of the Battle Creek Conference, Oct. 5 & 6, 1861,' *Review & Herald*, 8 October 1861, 148 (emphasis supplied).
7 'General Conference Proceedings,' *Review & Herald*, 20 November 1883, 732-733.
8 For details and references, see Pöhler, *Continuity and Change*, 191-196.
9 'If in anything it can be shown that what we hold in faith and practice is not according to the Bible, we are ready to modify it accordingly.' (Uriah Smith, 'In the Question Chair,' *Review & Herald*, 20 September 1892, 600)

The ambiguity arising from the continuing opposition to the formation of a creed and the simultaneous affirmation of a creedal statement persisted and increased in the twentieth century. While doctrinal rigidity and stagnation were opposed, the need for certain non-negotiable points of faith was upheld. The 'Fundamental Beliefs' published in the Church Manual since 1932 were looked upon as the official statement of the Adventist faith, and assent to it was regarded as a condition of church membership. In this way, differing interpretations of Bible teachings could be prevented, erroneous views and heresies be opposed, and non-negotiable teachings be defined. In other words, the Fundamental Beliefs statement served both to present the established faith of the church and to prevent opposing views from within.[10] In his book on the Apostles' Creed, W. R. Beach defended church creeds as a means of bringing about unity of faith, securing uniformity of teaching, and protecting against errors – benefits which Adventists had previously ascribed to the Bible and the prophetic gift (i.e., Ellen White).

In the 1970s, Adventists came closer than ever to attributing to their Fundamental Beliefs a criteriological function, ideally surpassed only by the Scriptures. When church leaders proposed a set of explanatory statements on certain controversial teachings (such as revelation/inspiration and creation/creationism), they evoked a heated controversy, particularly in North America. Reactions were both supportive and critical. Opposition came mainly from the academic community, which felt strongly inhibited by this move that would enable administrators, leaders, and controlling boards to evaluate the commitment to Adventism of current and prospective employees.[11] While many church members were supportive of the proposals to

---

[10] According to the *Church Manual* 'Denial of faith in the fundamentals of the gospel and in the cardinal doctrines of the church or teaching doctrines contrary to the same' is a sufficient reason for disfellowshipping (1951 ed., p. 224).

[11] W. J. Hackett, 'Preserve the Landmarks,' *Review & Herald*, 26 May 1977, 2.

protect the faith against erosion, others were concerned that it would bring the church dangerously close to becoming a creedal church.

With the acceptance of a newly written statement of Fundamental Beliefs at the General Conference Session in Dallas, in 1980, the Adventist church entered a new phase in its attitude toward 'creeds'. The strong opposition of the past had given way to a positive appreciation, which regarded the Fundamental Beliefs as a criterion of church membership and a reference point for defining Adventist faith. From then on, adherence to Adventism was more and more measured by someone's agreement, or lack of it, to the 28 Fundamental Beliefs. They serve as the benchmark of orthodoxy and the precondition of employment by church entities. Loyalty to the church is equated with full agreement to the '28 points'. This has led to a somewhat paradoxical situation. In order to be regarded as 'orthodox', what is explicitly stated in the 28 points of faith must not be questioned. On the other hand, what remains unsaid in that statement is regarded as non-binding. Thus, certain traditional teachings (such as the view on apocalyptic Babylon, the mark of the beast and other end-time events), which by many are regarded as 'present truth', have actually become adiaphora. On the other hand, any deviation from the officially voted text is viewed with suspicion.

Do Seventh-day Adventists have a binding, authoritative creed after all? Many in the church, including theologians, will affirm this and, beyond that, defend the importance of having such a declaration of faith. Thus, the question is not so much whether Adventists have, or need, a creedal statement but rather how detailed and explicit it should be and how it is actually being used by the church. A survey of Adventism's doctrinal history reveals a variety of confessional statements, differing from each other with respect to style (form), emphasis (content), and authority (function).

How Did the Adventist Fundamental Beliefs Develop?

The historical development of Adventists doctrines has been described in detail elsewhere.[12] Here the focus will be limited to the general direction that these developments have taken and the diverse manner in which Adventists have expressed the central points of their faith. There are at least five major trends, which will be briefly described in the following section.[13]

From Simple and Concise Statements to Detailed and Sophisticated Texts

From 1851 until 1938, the *Review & Herald* printed on its masthead the text of Rev 14:12 in order to express the Adventist faith in a nutshell. To early Sabbatarian Adventists, this implied obedience to the law of God and the teachings of Jesus, meaning the Old and New Testament *in toto*. More specifically, they focused on two doctrines, viz., the Sabbath and the Second Advent (including the sanctuary). When local congregations were organized in the 1860s, members signed a pledge 'covenanting to keep the commandments of God, and the faith of Jesus Christ.' In 1872, Uriah Smith published a 2,500-word 'Declaration' containing 25 'Fundamental Principles Taught and Practiced by the Seventh-day Adventists'. Texts of a similar kind were published in 1931/1932 and in 1980. The latter is the longest and most sophisticated creedal statement which the church has produced thus far. Its 27 (now 28) articles of faith reflect the expertise of the theologians who drafted the text.

From Non-Binding and Flexible to Authoritative and Precisely Worded Texts

In the preface to his Fundamental Principles, Uriah Smith emphasized that they were no 'articles of faith' or 'creed' having 'any authority' and were not 'designed to secure uniformity'. They merely

---

[12] See George R. Knight, *A Search for Identity: The Development of Seventh-day Adventist Beliefs* (Hagerstown, MD: Review and Herald, 2000); and Pöhler, *Continuity and Change*.

[13] For more details, see Pöhler, *Continuity and Change*, pp. 123-134.

stated what Adventists believed 'with great unanimity', providing a synopsis of the Adventist faith, the 'only object' of which was to accurately inform the public, correct erroneous views and prejudices, and distinguish Seventh-day Adventists from other Adventist groups. Even the 1931/1932 statement of Fundamental Beliefs was published without being officially voted by the church. However, in 1946, any future revisions of this text were made dependent on a formal vote by a General Conference session, thereby giving *post ex facto* recognition to it by the church. The declaration of 1980, in turn, went through a long process of preparation, discussion, and revision before it was voted at a plenary session. The changes of 2015 went through an even more extended and elaborate process than that.[14] The newly revised Fundamental Beliefs Statement will likely be considered more official, binding and authoritative than ever.

From Adventist Distinctives to Christian Fundamentals

If one compares the Synopsis of Uriah Smith with later summary statements, the change from 'heterodox' to 'orthodox' teachings is evident. While Smith rejected the doctrine of the Trinity, the classical Christian teaching on the nature of Christ and the atonement, and also proposed a heterodox view on the 'new birth', later statements reflected some noteworthy changes in Adventist beliefs. In addition, recent confessional statements reveal a shift from an earlier emphasis on distinctive doctrines (law, judgment) to an accentuation of basic Christian teachings (salvation by grace through faith). Closely related to this is the move away from the law-centred (and even legalistic) thinking of the early decades to a more Christ-centred approach, focusing on the Gospel and offering believers assurance of salvation, even in view of a pre-Advent judgment.

---

[14] The procedure started in 2010 and gave all church members an opportunity to make suggestions regarding the rewording of the 28 articles. See 'Statement of Fundamental Beliefs – A Living Document,' *Reflections – The BRI Newsletter*, 2 October 2011; and 'Listening, Studying, and Sharing,' *Adventist World*, 6 April 2012.

From Focusing on the Future to Paying Attention to the Present

One significant side-effect of the increasing concentration on the gospel message was a decreasing emphasis on the apocalyptic focus of (post-) Millerite Adventism. It resulted from a deeper understanding of New Testament eschatology, characterised by a tension between the completed salvation through the death and resurrection of Jesus ('already') and the final consummation of the kingdom of God at the coming of Christ ('not yet'). While upholding the future-oriented teachings of the church (final events, the millennium, the new earth), the 1980 declaration gives increased attention to the present time and its challenges: care for the environment, stewardship of the earth, marriage and family, healthful living, social relations, etc. The traditional emphasis on 'last things' has been supplemented by a growing concern for the penultimate things.

From an Apologetic and Polemical Approach to a Positive Christian Stance

When Uriah Smith wrote his Synopsis of the Advent faith, the church was engaged in theological debates with Christians of other denominations. It is no surprise, therefore, that the Declaration of 1872 was also engaged in opposing erroneous views and even attacking other denominations, while presenting the Sabbath-keepers as the only true Adventists who are being faithful to the teachings of the Bible. In the spirit of his time, Smith polemicised against the 'the papal power, with all its abominations' (#8) and noted that the 'the man of sin, the papacy ... has mislead almost all Christendom' (#13). In the 1931/1932 Declaration, no accusations were raised against other denominations. Later, L. E. Froom noted that 'the old largely negative approach – emphasizing chiefly the things wherein we differ from all other religious groups – is past, definitely past. And that is as it should be.'[15] Likewise, the 1980 Statement of Fundamental Beliefs is free from any polemical and apologetic overtones, presenting

---

[15] L. E. Froom, 'New Approaches Imperative for a New Day,' *Ministry*, March 1966, 10-13.

Adventist beliefs on the basis of biblical and theological reasoning alone. While this may be seen as evidence of the progressive maturing of Adventism, others may look upon it as a sign of the gradual loss of distinctive Adventist identity.[16]

In looking upon these developments it becomes clear that Seventh-day Adventism is sharing in the same processes that other Christian churches have experienced before. Beginning as a small movement with loose structures and beliefs still in the making, they gradually grow into large, well-organised denominations that find it judicious to define and refine their beliefs more narrowly and minutely until they become settled teachings cast in theological concrete. This process may largely be inescapable. The very success of a movement – its growth, expansion, and diversification – calls for a clear profile that helps preserve its identity. The homogeneous character of the incipient movement gradually gives way to a heterogeneous body of believers who no longer share the same intellectual framework, social imprint, cultural context, or behavior and lifestyle. In order to keep their church united in faith, leaders tend to resort to creeds or confessional statements that define the boundaries of the community and thus strengthen its cohesiveness.

Benefits and Ill Effects of Creedal Statements

Undeniably, there are benefits in having a creed. At the same time, there also seem to be serious risks in producing such statements, as John Loughborough had forcibly argued back in 1861. This section of the essay looks at the advantages and disadvantages of creedal statements from an Adventist viewpoint. What are the benefits and drawbacks of such authoritative texts? To keep the survey brief and

---

[16] For quite a few Adventists and Adventist groups, to criticise the numerous errors and deceptions of end-time Babylon is seen as an essential part of preaching the 'eternal gospel' as presented in Rev 14. One may wonder, therefore, to what extent the stance of 1980 has taken hold of the thinking of the church at large.

concise, only a listing of the 'boon and bane' of creeds will be provided here.

On the positive side: Confessional statements provide a summary of the core beliefs of a church and explain them to insiders and outsiders alike. They are a united expression of the community's faith convictions that fosters its identity and 'the unity of the faith' (Eph 4:13). A common confession belongs to the essence of the Christian faith. It gives a clear and concise testimony to the world about the beliefs of the church and answers the call of the apostle who admonished believers: 'Always be ready to make your defense to anyone who demands from you an accounting for the hope that is in you' (1 Pet 3:15).[17] They help protect the church against misinterpretations and misrepresentations of its beliefs and save it from being 'tossed to and fro and blown about by every wind of doctrine' (Eph 4:14).

On the negative side: Creeds reflect a particular phase and level of understanding, which tends to be canonised and, consequently, impedes further growth, advancement or possible correction of the understanding and expression of the faith. In this way, today's 'present truth' may become an impediment to tomorrow's 'new light'. Usually, creeds are treated as criteria of orthodoxy/heresy and as instruments to marginalise non-conformist members. Rather than serving as a descriptive tool, they are used prescriptively to ostracise and even expel dissidents. Having been formulated in a specific historical and cultural context, they may lose their timeliness in a changing world and become unsuitable in different religious and cultural environments. For all intents and purposes, they take the place of the Bible, which ostensibly is 'the only rule of faith and practice' for Adventist Christians. This stands in sharp contrast to the conviction of the pioneers of the church.

---

[17] It was a request from the African Union for an official statement that could be used in talking to state authorities that prompted the drafting and publishing of the 1931/1932 Statement of Fundamental Beliefs.

Part 2
Features and Functions of an Adventist 'Creed'

After this historical review and analysis of Adventist attitudes toward creedal statements, including their pros and cons, the second part of this essay will approach the subject in a theologically constructive manner. On the premise that some kind of creedal statement is useful and even desirable, the question needs to be asked: What characteristics should such a statement of belief possess? Rather than proposing particular points of faith, this essay is concerned with the properties of a meaningful and consistent 'creed' that is suitable for confessing the Adventist Christian faith in today's multicultural world. After proposing ten features of such a creedal statement, we will focus attention on the recent revisions of the 28 Fundamental Beliefs and their significance.

Desirable Features of an Adventist 'Creed'

The following summary contains both formal and substantial aspects of a creed. It is a kind of 'wish list' that can be used as a criterion for evaluating creedal statements.

'Brevity is the Soul of Wit'

Rather than presenting detailed and elaborate explanations, a confession of faith should be as brief and concise as possible. Less is more – this insight may well be applicable here. A handful of paragraphs or articles fitting on a single page would suffice. The current Adventist Statement of Fundamental Beliefs encompasses a whopping 4,200 words, making it far too cumbersome to be memorised or recited in public. On the other hand, it is a carefully crafted and useful tool for studying Adventist doctrines in some detail.

Focus on Essentials

A Christian confession consists of fundamental statements of faith. It should focus on weighty matters, leaving less important issues aside. Points of faith need to be weighed, not merely counted. This calls for a deliberate distinction between central and peripheral issues. This is not to argue for a watered-down creed that evades the harder points of faith. But without such a differentiation, peripheral issues are paid too much attention. Adventist faith is holistic, encompassing all aspects of life. Still, there are essentials and non-essentials (cf. Matt 23:23; Rom 14:17). Traditionally, dogmatic theology focuses on three main themes: God (including the Trinity), man (including sin), and salvation (including the new life, the church, and eschatology). A well-balanced statement of faith will focus on these central themes and integrate them one way or the other in its portrayal.

Trinitarian Structure

Ancient Christian creeds are characterised by a Trinitarian structure. In the early decades, Seventh-day Adventists strongly opposed a Trinitarian faith; later, they revised their view. While Adventist declarations of Fundamental Beliefs do not follow a Trinitarian outline, such an approach might be appropriate. In this case, however, there is the challenge of integrating all important points into a threefold scheme. Traditional Christian creeds attach such crucial topics as the church, forgiveness of sin, resurrection, and eternal life to the third article on the Holy Spirit while omitting the question of Christian discipleship altogether. Thus, a Trinitarian structure requires careful drafting so that nothing of importance is left out by allocating everything that is said to the triune God.

Christ-Centeredness

Of greater importance than a Trinitarian structure is the Christ-centeredness of an Adventist statement of faith. According to *Seventh-day Adventists Believe ...*, all Adventist doctrines are Christ-centered and should be understood in relationship to Him.[18] However, it is one thing to make this claim and another to answer it. While there may be no agreement on whether the former and current confessional statements fully comply with it, nearly everyone will agree to this ideal. Christ is the foundation, centre and reference point of all Adventist teaching and the focus of all truths of faith. At heart, a Christian creed is a confession of faith in Christ, the living Word of God. Thus, every doctrine should foster a better understanding of the meaning of the confession to Christ as Lord.[19]

Testimonial Character

A confession is a personal or shared affirmation of faith which is most properly expressed in the first-person singular or plural. While neutral language in the third person has the ring of objectivity and factuality ('There will be a resurrection of the dead'), the subjective form ('I believe/we believe in the resurrection of the dead') more closely corresponds to the nature of a confession. Rather than making a compelling case for what is being asserted, it testifies in a personal manner to a truth accepted by faith. The church may *teach* doctrines, but only people can *believe* and *confess* them. In other

---

[18] *Seventh-day Adventists Believe* (Silver Spring, MD: Gen. Conf. of SDAs, Ministerial Assn., 2005), pp. vii-ix.

[19] In 1905, at a conference of the German Union, an unusual set of Fundamental Beliefs *(Glaubensgrundsätze)* was printed in the conference brochure. It related all doctrinal assertions to Christ himself by using phrases like 'his glorious gospel [atonement, life in Christ],' 'his law of love [Decalogue],' 'his day of rest [Sabbath],' 'his gifts of the holy Spirit,' 'his divine plan [tithing],' 'his counsel as the true physician [health, abstinence],' 'his attitude towards authorities [state, taxes]' and 'his prophetic word.' In this way, the Christ-centered nature of the Adventist faith became very conspicuous. To this author's knowledge, this was a singular approach.

words, a confession is not an incontestable line of argument but the act of professing one's faith. While 'creed' or 'fundamental principles of faith' refer to a written statement, 'confession' denotes the act of acknowledging Christ. Only in a secondary sense does it refer to the content of the 'confession'. For this reason, a creed should also refrain from attacking the faith convictions of other people or communities. A claim to objective truth can be controverted by factual evidence. A credo, on the other hand, must be acknowledged for what it is – a confession by a person or group to a reality accessible only by faith. While Uriah Smith engaged in explicit polemics against the papacy in 1872, more recent Adventist faith statements have refrained from it. Neither should a statement of faith take an overtly apologetic stance. To witness to the truth does not require self-justification, for a credo is not about us but about God. There is no need for either an aggressive or a defensive posture – unless the church finds itself *in statu confessionis* when its very existence is at stake.[20]

Biblical Terminology

In order to remain true to the biblical witness, it is judicious to follow the language of the Scriptures rather closely in presenting the truths of faith. This reduces the risk of deviating from the intended meaning of Bible teachings and misinterpreting its message. It is the strength of the 28 Fundamental Beliefs that the theologians who wrote them consistently followed this principle. While being theologically informed, the statements are generally couched in biblical terminology and can thus be understood by everyone familiar

---

[20] In 1934, the Confessional Synod of the German Evangelical Church met in Barmen to withstand the 'German Christians' who had aligned themselves with the ideological views of the Nazi state. The Barmen Declaration not only reiterated the historic Protestant faith in the form of six 'evangelical truths' but also countered false doctrines reflecting the Nazi ideology. Inasmuch as the very foundation of the Christian faith – the gospel of Jesus Christ as attested in the Scriptures – and the survival of the church was at stake, the Barmen Declaration pronounced seven times, 'We reject the false doctrine.' In this extreme case, the polemic against the wolves in sheep's clothing was needed in order to unmask the seductive approach of the German Reichskirche.

with the Bible, independent of one's own cultural background. In addition, using biblical terminology is a tacit acknowledgment of the sola scriptura principle. On the other hand, to use (Western) contemporary language and reasoning in presenting and defending biblical truths may not be advisable or beneficial in a culturally diverse church and world.

Scripture-Boundedness (scripturality)

For a church that upholds the sola-scriptura principle it goes without saying that its credo will submit to the final authority of the written Word of God. This is the unquestioned position of Seventh-day Adventists and is clearly expressed in the Preamble to the Fundamental Beliefs.[21] However, to consider the Fundamental Beliefs binding and authoritative, too, may lead to a conflict between these two authorities. This is not just a theoretical risk as can be illustrated from the Church Manual. The alternative Baptismal Vow contains only three questions, the second of which reads as follows: 'Do you accept the *teachings of the Bible* as expressed in the *Statement of Fundamental Beliefs* of the Seventh-day Adventist Church, and do you pledge by God's grace to live your life in harmony with *these teachings?* (Emphasis supplied).[22] It is not clear whether *these teachings* refer to the Bible or to the Fundamental Beliefs. It is even less certain that those who answer in the affirmative all have a clear understanding of the crucial difference between the two. It would, therefore, be judicious to reword this sentence in order to make its meaning crystal clear to all.[23]

---

[21] 'Seventh-day Adventists accept the Bible as their only creed and hold certain fundamental beliefs to be the teachings of the Holy Scriptures.' (cf. art. 1 and 18)

[22] *Seventh-day Adventist Church Manual*, 18th ed. 2010, 47.

[23] The German Church Manual has clarified the meaning of the sentence in this way: '…and do you want to live according to *the teachings of the Bible*.' (Emphasis supplied) 'Nimmst du die Lehren der Bibel an, wie sie in den Glaubensüberzeugungen der Siebenten-Tags-Adventisten zum Ausdruck kommen, und möchtest du dich mit Gottes Hilfe nach den *Weisungen des Wortes Gottes* richten?' (*Gemeindeordnung* 2012:61; Emphasis supplied)

Identity Markers (traditionality)

If a church desires to retain its unique identity, its credo must not only present the historic beliefs of the Christian church in general but also express the distinctive teachings of the denomination. Only then will it serve as a unifying tool that helps protect and strengthen the collective identity. These distinctives are usually related to certain experiences that had a lasting impact on the faith and/or practice of a community. They are part of the denomination's collective memory and form its special tradition. In the case of Seventh-day Adventists, three such experiences stand out and are even reflected in the church's name: the Millerite movement, the 'remnant' experience, and the rediscovery of the Sabbath. The distinctive teachings that grew out of these experiences have been developed further and constitute crucial identity markers for an Adventist credo: The Sabbath as a divine gift for mankind, the advent hope as an energizing force, and the Adventist church as a worldwide family of faith. With these core beliefs, an Adventist credo may indeed have a unifying effect on the church.

Cultural Relevance (contemporaneity)

Besides acknowledging the authority of the Bible and honouring the church's tradition, a creedal statement must also be relevant and applicable to the society in which the believers are living. It is not enough therefore to repeat the fundamental teachings of the Bible and to keep the distinctive insights of previous generations alive. A credo must also relate to the intellectual and practical challenges of living in the here and now. While the Fundamental Beliefs of earlier times had little to say on mundane questions, the Statement of 1980 and its later addendum reveal a growing awareness of the need to address actual life questions that have a direct bearing on the faith.[24]

---

[24] For example, responsibility for the environment is addressed in art. 6 and 7, non-discrimination is treated in art. 14, while marriage/family and child education are discussed in art. 23.

Open-Endedness

Finally, a creed should never be written on stone but always on paper. This is to say that it should remain open to change, improvement, and correction. While the historic Christian creeds constitute fixed declarations that are not subject to changes, the Adventist credo may be revised if the need for it arises. After all, a confession of faith is not the ultimate truth but merely an authentic witness to it. As such it should be considered open-ended and treated as descriptive and informative rather than as prescriptive and normative. How else could the Bible de facto be 'the only creed'?

The Changing Role of the Fundamental Beliefs

The General Conference of San Antonio

In July of 2015, the General Conference session in San Antonio, Texas, discussed and voted editorial revisions of the Fundamental Beliefs, originally adopted in 1980. Its 27 articles had been enlarged by a 28th paragraph in 2005 (art. 11). At the General Conference session in 2010, a 'Fundamental Beliefs Review Committee' (FBRC) had been set up in order (1) to review the statement and suggest revised wordings and (2) to integrate article 6 and the 'Response to "An Affirmation of Creation"' that had been adopted by the Annual Council of the General Conference Executive Committee in 2004. Between October 2011 and October 2012, the FBRC solicited suggestions from church members generally.[25] It then sorted through some 200 suggestions and prepared a preliminary draft that was presented at the 2013 Annual Council. After further refinement, a final draft was voted at the Annual Council in 2014 to be sent to the

---

[25] The call to make suggestions regarding the rewording of the Fundamental Beliefs was explicitly extended to all church members as individuals, not to theologians, scholars, institutions or committees. The FBRC was made up of three Old Testament scholars (Artur Steele, Angel Rodriguez, Gerhard Pfandl) and editor Bill Knott.

General Conference session in 2015.[26] The rationale for this review process was taken from the preamble of the Fundamental Beliefs statement, which reads:

> Seventh-day Adventists accept the Bible as their only creed and hold certain fundamental beliefs to be the teaching of the Holy Scriptures. These beliefs, as set forth here, constitute the church's understanding and expression of the teaching of Scripture. *Revision of these statements may be expected* at a General Conference session when the church is led by the Holy Spirit to a fuller understanding of Bible truth or finds better language in which to express the teachings of God's Holy Word. (Emphasis supplied)

This reference is noteworthy inasmuch as the book *Seventh-day Adventists Believe* does not have a chapter on the Preamble, which a number of Adventists regard as the most important part of the entire statement. It seems that the Preamble had long been considered somewhat delicate because of its apparent openness to doctrinal change and revision. More recently, however, the Preamble was appealed to in order to warrant the proposed revisions. At the same time, and in order to avert suspicion that the church was changing its historic beliefs, the proposed adaptations were said to be modifications without substantive change. BRI director Artur Stele declared: 'All the so-called changes to the 28 Fundamental Beliefs are really not changing anything in which we have believed.'[27] Stele justified the proposed modifications with linguistic improvements because of changing definitions of words (such as 'marriage') as well as with the goal of clarifying previous statements and preventing wrong or unwanted interpretations (ibid.).

---

[26] http://www.adventistreview.org/assets/public/news/2014-10/Fundamental_Beliefs_Statement-last_version.

[27] Artur Stele, 'What About the Upcoming GC Session?' *Reflections* [BRI Newsletter], 2 July 2015.

Most of the changes were of an editorial nature: avoiding repetitions, correcting punctuation, substituting supporting Bible references etc. Noteworthy is the inclusive language that is now being used throughout the document. It reveals a growing sensitivity for 'just language' and a genuine concern for gender equality and justice. This indicates that the church is willing and able to respond positively to cultural shifts and societal developments. This applies also to the substitution of 'guide' for 'disciplinarian' in the context of child education and the mention of 'both single and married persons' as members of the church (art. 23). Likewise, the call to minister compassionately 'to the physical, mental, social, emotional, and spiritual needs of humanity' (art. 11) reflects a growing sense of responsibility towards the world.

More conspicuous and significant, however, are the revisions that redefine certain beliefs so as to render impossible any reading that could be seen as an accommodation to contemporary thought. For instance, article 23 now calls marriage three times a union between 'a man and a woman', while the previous version had used the terms '(marriage) partners' to avoid such repetition. In this way, any reinterpretation of 'marriage' is to be pre-empted. The same applies to the word 'bodily' added to the phrase 'the resurrection of Christ' (art. 9) and the annotation of the Genesis flood by the phrase 'as presented in the historical account of Genesis 1-11' (art. 8).

The most important change, however, is found in article 6, which deals with creation. Its purpose is to make impossible any interpretation of the Genesis creation story in terms of theistic evolution, a view that is held by some Adventists, particularly in the scientific community. At the 2004 Annual Council, a 'Response to the Affirmation of Creation' had been accepted and voted that emphasised 'a literal, recent, six-day creation' taking place in six 'literal 24-hour days'.[28] According to a vote by the 2010 General Conference Session, this notion was to be integrated into the Fundamental Beliefs statement. The revised part of article 6 now reads as follows:

> God has revealed in Scripture the authentic and *historical* account of His creative activity. He created the universe, and in *a recent six-day creation* the Lord made 'the heavens and the earth, the sea, and all that is in them' and rested on the seventh day. Thus He established the Sabbath as a perpetual memorial of the work He performed and completed during *six literal days* that together with the Sabbath constituted *the same unit of time that we call a week today.* (Emphasis supplied)

The newly added phrases say in no uncertain terms how the biblical witness to creation is to be understood by Adventists: as a historical, recent, literal event lasting seven 24-hour days. The text is taking great pains to disallow any view that is not in full agreement with this strict definition. Clearly, the revisions do not intend to build bridges of understanding to people outside the church. Rather, they are geared toward church members entertaining doubts regarding the creationist view. Are they supposed to be put off and scared away?[29]

---

[28] The document 'Affirmation of Creation' was the product of the 2002-2004 Faith and Science Conferences, which explored the scientific and theological aspects of the creation-evolution debate and gave Adventist scholars of various fields an opportunity to discuss openly conflicting interpretations of Gen 1-11.

[29] The same impression was created by the Sabbath School Quarterly on Origins during the first quarter of 2013. It stressed the necessity of believing in a historical, literal, recent six-day creation, the incompatibility between Adventism and theistic evolution, and the impossibility and 'logical absurdity' of mediating between the two. Never before has a Sabbath School Quarterly been used so overtly to stigmatise church members who are entertaining divergent views. 'What, then, could be more tragic, or a deeper fall from faith, than for those professing to be members of that [SDA] church to argue in favor of evolution?' (Sabbath School Lesson Quarterly, 15 March 2013)

Whatever the intent, this approach recalls the concern and warning that John Loughborough had expressed back in 1861.

There are some other editorial revisions trying to clarify certain points of doctrine and ward off unorthodox interpretations. Regarding the Holy Spirit, it is said that 'he is as much a person as are the Father and the Son' (art. 5). It is debateable whether the term 'person' is helpful or rather inept. The article on 'Christ's Ministry in the Heavenly Sanctuary' (art. 23) codifies a typological reading of the Old Testament sanctuary that has been questioned by Adventists on exegetical and theological grounds. Again, it is hard to avoid the impression that this change intends to put a final stop to a debate that has been going on for decades. Will the Statement of Fundamental Beliefs be used as a normative Adventist creed after all?

On the other hand, Adventists still seem to be willing to abandon inappropriate doctrinal claims. For instance, Christ's coming is no longer said to be 'imminent' but rather 'near' – a more appropriate biblical term (art. 25). This is also demonstrated by article 18 dealing with the gift of prophecy. This article had called the writings of Ellen G. White 'a continuing and authoritative source of truth.' In view of the Roman Catholic teaching on the two sources of revelation (Scripture and tradition), this phrase was inappropriate to express confidence in White's prophetic ministry. It took the church thirty-five years to find a more fitting expression: 'Her writings speak with prophetic authority.' Article 18 now also avoids the claim that *the Bible* teaches that Ellen White had the gift of prophecy. This view is now relativised as something 'we [*Adventists*] believe'. In addition, the Holy Scriptures are said to be the 'supreme' and 'definitive' revelation of God's will, thereby strengthening the primacy and supreme authority of the Bible for Adventist faith and practice (art. 1).

Quo vadis, Adventism?

As was to be expected, the delegates to the 2015 General Conference responded affirmatively to the proposed revisions. With a large majority, they accepted the proposal of the leadership to codify the traditional Adventist language and teaching in order to protect the exclusive identity and mission of the Adventist church. This lies behind the restrictive language of several of the proposed changes. If this trend continues, it will increasingly polarise the world church and lead to the marginalisation of more open-minded and critical church members. It is to be feared that this will cause quite a few to leave the church or go into inner emigration. It will also deter others from joining it in the first place. An outward and/or inward differentiation may strengthen the unity of the 'remnant', but it entails the risk of regressing into a more sectarian mode of thought. Only time will reveal which trend will prevail in the long run and how the Seventh-day Adventist church – particularly its younger generation – will respond to the challenges of the secular and postmodern world.

Whether the recent adaptations of the Fundamental Beliefs statement are considered marginal or significant is open to debate. Of much more importance, however, is the changing role of these modifications, which constitutes an absolute novelty in the history of the denomination. Never before were changes in the Fundamental Beliefs justified – let alone explicitly – by the necessity of making impossible within the church any deviating interpretations of Biblical statements.[30] As a result, the hoped-for unity of faith may turn out to be a uniformity of expression, leaving little room for an individual's thought and conscience. A mature faith will not grow in such a climate.

---

[30] 'These revisions leave no room for doubt about what we believe as Seventh-day Adventists, no room for equivocation, no room for waffling.' (Clinton Whalen, 'In the Beginning ... God', *Adventist World*, 15 September 2015)

In this context, the issue of the binding nature of the Adventist 'creed' needs to be addressed. No one will deny that its authority is derived from, and subject to, the Scriptures. This implies that at baptism we become committed, not to 28 Fundamental Beliefs, but to Christ and the teachings of the Bible, reflected by the confessional statement. Only in this way can the Scriptures retain their superior authority as 'the only rule of faith and practice'. Thus, a creed must be read and interpreted in the light of Scripture, rather than Scripture being read and interpreted in the light of a fixed creed. Theological disputes are to be settled, not by referring to a creed, but by reference to the Word of God. The teachings of the Bible have priority over against their interpretations by a creed. 'The Statement of Fundamental Beliefs is really the church's reading and reception of Scripture and it is authoritative only to the extent that it accurately depicts the message of Scripture.'[31] Even if one concedes to the Fundamental Beliefs 'a legitimate juridical role in settling doctrinal disputes,'[32] this does not make them the final arbiter of truth. After all, a judge is subject to the law that he is supposed to uphold. In a similar manner, while a creed interprets the Bible, it is subordinate to it.

Much will depend, therefore, on how the church understands the authority and function of its Fundamental Beliefs: as an established creed that protects the doctrinal traditions from challenges from without or within, or as an expression of the community's dynamic faith that remains open to new insights deriving from biblical study, theological reflection, and contemporary world experience. To opt for 'present truth' entails the challenge to avoid rigid dogmatism (where all believe what is prescribed) as much as indifferent relativism (where all believe what they like). Adventists should resist the temptation to codify their beliefs in a way that stifles growth while learning

---

[31] Kwabena Donkor, 'Role of Fundamental Beliefs in the Church', in *Message, Mission, and Unity of the Church,* Studies in Adventist Ecclesiology, vol. 2, ed. by Angel Manuel Rodríguez (Silver Spring, MD: General Conference of SDAs, Biblical Research Institute, 2013), 295, 287-302

[32] Ibid., 298

to express their faith in ways that appeal to people with different intellectual, cultural, and religious backgrounds. Only then will the Adventist 'creed' truly be a confession of faith. 'Credo – I believe....'

In sum, this essay suggests that a common confession of faith is essential to the Christian faith and indispensable for the Adventist witness to the world. On the other hand, a creedal set of beliefs, serving as a binding rule of faith that minutely defines doctrines and is used in disciplining members, is ill-advised and should be avoided. The church needs to steer clear of the Scylla of dogmatic indifferentism and relativism as well as the Charybdis of creedalism and dogmatic fixation. In this way, it will honour the old adage "ecclesia reformata semper reformanda".

Towards a Scripture-Based Theology

Gunnar Pedersen

The Reformation challenge has been summarised in the sentence *Ecclesia reformata semper reformanda,* that is, the need for the church to continually learn and unlearn. For the Reformers this quest focused directly on the Scriptures as the *norma normata* for Christian beliefs and practice in contrast to medieval epistemology. By adopting a *sola scriptura* principle, the Reformation tradition thus broadly defined its epistemological source of authority for Christian beliefs and practice that in turn called for a revision of hermeneutics. They abandoned the medieval fourfold hermeneutics by limiting it to the literal sense (*Sensus Literalis*) of Scriptures. They further sharpened this hermeneutical principle by arguing for the clarity of Scriptures and thus for the Scriptures to be its own interpreter. In other words they made the revolutionary claim that a hermeneutics for reading the Scriptures must arise out the thematic, logic and literary structures of the scriptural texts themselves.

However, the question remains whether these broad hermeneutical principles fully resolve the hermeneutical challenge of how to let Scripture be its own interpreter. Their new hermeneutical focus clearly necessitates a reliable insight into the nature and function of language in human thinking, communication and interpretation and thus the ideological perspectives of both author and reader. Many challenging insights and theories regarding human language and thinking have emerged since the time of the Reformers that have complicated what initially might have appeared as a simple straightforward plain reading of the Scriptures. The subsequent schools of hermeneutics have often ruled out the possibility of arriving at a unified biblical theology.[1] However, if a unified biblical theology is not possible then the Scriptures as the sole ground of doctrinal formulations is virtually ruled out and any attempt to systematise its teachings is an exercise in futility. Even to imagine that the biblical material contains a coherent worldview paradigm is an intellectual illusion. Thus the epistemological ambition of the sixteenth century Reformers to base their systematic theology on the Scriptures alone appears to be a dead end street. The need therefore to discover and formulate a biblically-based hermeneutics for reading and applying the teachings of the Scriptures remains an ongoing and urgent quest within this tradition. The aim of this chapter is to search for a macro-hermeneutics that might transcend the present hermeneutical impasse. This search is propelled by the growing contemporary insight into the narrative nature of the Scriptural texts; an insight that opens up new possibilities for allowing the biblical material to tell its own story on its own premises while avoiding the pitfall of imposing the reader's own perspective on the texts. The search will thus attempt to clarify the reading processes and premises on which a coherent biblical theology may be articulated as the basis for a coherent systematic theology.

The mental process of moving from the biblical text to system[2] is not an optional human activity but arises out of the practical existential

---

[1] For an overview of the issues and challenges implied in the contemporary hermeneutical debates see: Anthony C. Thiselton, *Hermeneutics, An introduction* (Grand Rapids, MI: William B. Eerdmans, 2009); Anthony C. Thiselton, *Thiselton on Hermeneutics, the Collected Works and New Essays of Anthony Thiselton* (Aldershot, Hampshire: Ashgate, 2006); Anthony Thiselton, *the Hermeneutics of Doctrine* (Grand Rapids, MI: William B. Eerdmans, 2007). See also: Moises Silva, *Foundations of Contemprary Interpretation* (Leicester; Apollos, 1996).

[2] In this article the term 'system' is applied as a reference to the human comprehension of the biblical themes as a coherent system of thought.

needs of the readers of the scriptural texts. The real choice is not whether one will engage in textual exegesis and theological reflections and applications, but whether one will do this in an unreflected fashion or in a careful methodical manner.³ While a topical approach to Scripture naturally arises from the practical existential, mental and pedagogical needs of the canonical readers and audiences, this chapter will argue that the process of reaching any topical formulation and systematic application of the themes of Scripture should be based on a transparent biblical theology.

Fernando Canale in a series of articles has proposed a resolution to the methodological challenge of proceeding from text to system as he explores the limits and potentials of textual exegesis and systematic constructions as currently understood and practiced within the Seventh-day Adventist tradition.⁴ He observes that for Evangelicals, including Seventh-day Adventists, the practice of textual exegesis is mainly equated with doing biblical theology. According to his critical observation, the current methods of textual exegesis are not designed to search for the biblical metanarrative or worldview so essential for a systematic construction of a coherent system of thought. Thus there is a hermeneutical gap between the inductive activity of textual exegesis and the deductive activity of systematic reflections. His concern is rooted in his awareness that systematics is more than a summary and organisation of the parts of textual exegesis as suggested by the

---

3   Wayne Grudem states that 'the necessity of systematic theology for teaching what the Bible says comes about primarily because we are finite in our memory and in the amount of time at our disposal.' Wayne Grudem, p. 27.
4   Fernando Canale, 'From vision to System: Finishing the Task of Adventist Biblical and Systematic Theologies – Part I', *Journal of the Adventist Theological Society*, 15/2 (Autumn 2004), 5-39; Fernando Canale, 'From vision to System: Finishing the Task of Adventist Biblical and Systematic Theologies – Part II', *Journal of the Adventist Theological Society*, 16/1-2 (Autumn 2005), 114-142; Fernando Canale, 'From vision to System: Finishing the Task of Adventist Biblical and Systematic Theologies – Part III', *Journal of the Adventist Theological Society*, 17/12 (Autumn 2006), 114-142.

evangelical scholars such as Wayne Grudem and Millard Erickson.[5] Canale argues that textual exegesis needs to be supplemented with the methods of systematics in order to discover the deeper biblical metanarrative or worldview necessary for understanding the Scriptures as a coherent belief system.[6]

In support of this thesis he refers to the pioneering work of Norman Gully that in his view is 'the first true systematic theology to come from an Adventist hand.' Canale argues that according to Gully a canonically based systematics needs the 'hermeneutical guide of the biblical metanarrative,' or 'worldview' as necessary for understanding it as a coherent belief system. Canale argues that for Gully 'the biblical metanarrative operates as a guiding light orienting our interpretation of Scripture and biblical doctrine. It also identifies and "corrects any interpretation that does not fit in with the biblical worldview." Finally, it guides us in understanding the inner logic of biblical thinking.'[7] He adds: 'Gully correctly concludes, "the center of a theological system must be the same as the underlying center of Scripture, if the system is to be true to Scripture." In this way the, the centers of biblical and systematic theology are identical.'[8]

I fully concur with the observation that the biblical metanarrative or worldview has critical macro-hermeneutical significance for a Scripture-based theology and for its systematic articulation and application. I further concur that the centre of a theological system must be the same as the underlying centre of Scripture if theology is to operate within the horizon of the canon. I agree with Canale that textual exegesis by itself seems insufficient to bridge the gap between text and system and that there is a missing methodical link

---

[5] Fernando Canale, 'From vision to System: Finishing the Task of Adventist Biblical and Systematic Theologies – Part II', *Journal of the Adventist Theological Society,* 15/1-2 (Autumn 2005), 135. See also Canale, 119.
[6] Canale, 126-38.
[7] Canale, 135.
[8] Canale, 135-36.

within the current process. Traditionally philosophy provided the metanarrative through which the biblical material was ordered as a system of thought. However, Canale rejects this approach, arguing that it is through the constructive approach of systematic theology that the biblical metanarrative is retrieved. However, in this chapter it will be proposed that the impasse lies precisely in the current perception of the roles of textual exegesis and systematic construction and that neither process retrieves the biblical metanarrative by itself.[9] Thus if the biblical metanarrative so critical for macro-hermeneutics is not retrieved purely by the process of exegesis nor by the process of systematics, by what means is it then discovered?

There is a need to sharpen the awareness of the inductive and deductive processes by which we consciously or unconsciously think and thus revision or re-map the methodological process by which the reader mentally moves from text to system. Methodologically I will suggest a triple methodical process beginning with *textual exegesis*, proceeding through a *thematic analysis* and ending in *systematic application*. Unfortunately the activity of thematic analysis and exposition both in part and as a whole is frequently sidelined or neglected, and thus appears as a missing link in the mental process of proceeding from text to system. Even when thematic analysis is recognised as a necessary link between text and system, it is not always granted a critical bridging hermeneutical role. The inductive/deductive process of proceeding through a thematic analysis of the

---

[9] Canale says: 'Besides, the biblical text does not yield its metanarrative to the descriptive approach of biblical theology, but the constructive approach of systematic theology.' He adds: 'The biblical meta-narrative comes to view when we are able to follow the inner logic and progression of the historical process of divine activities described in scripture.' However, the latter is the outcome of a thematic analysis of Scripture that I will argue is best categorised as biblical theology proper constituting a link between exegesis and systematics. Fernando Canale, 'From vision to System: Finishing the Task of Adventist Biblical and Systematic Theologies – Part III', *Journal of the Adventist Theological Society*, 17/12 (Autumn 2006), 58-9.

Scripture will for the purpose of this chapter be defined as biblical theology. Before further defining the methodological steps in the search for a hermeneutics for a Scripture-based theology, the need for the discipline of biblical theology as the bridge between the biblical text and theological system needs further consideration.

The Need for a Biblical Theology

It is generally recognised that the biblical canon is composed of micro and macro stories, but it is not agreed that such stories assume a grand metanarrative.[10] However, while the Bible appears to be the end product of a long and complex historical process, 'the end product needs to be examined in its own right'.[11] Several scholars, such as Breward Childs, James Barr, James Sanders and others, have called for a reassessment of the approach to biblical theology. N. T. Wright and others, such as Craig Bartholomew and Michael Goheen, have addressed the issue by proposing that the biblical text actually forms a grand historical narrative proceeding in stages; a narrative that must be understood from the inside of its own worldview logic in order for its meaning to be to unlocked.[12]

Their thesis is that all humans inhabit a 'story' as an ideological frame of reference or worldview first principles. This serves as a mental lens through which they see and experience and interpret the empirical world; it informs their values and actions, and through it they understand and assign meaning to historic events. Unless the biblical world of thought is an exception to this general cultural phenomenon, the biblical authors inhabit a metanarrative or

---

[10] Walter C. Kaiser Jr., *Recovering the Unity of the Bible: One continuous Story, Plan and Purpose* (Grand Rapids, MI: Zondervan, 2009), pp. 11-24.

[11] G. W. Stroup, *The Promise of Narrative Theology: Recovering the Gospel in the Church* (Atlanta: John Knox Press, 1981), pp. 145.

[12] Craig Bartholomew & Michael Goheen, Scripture & Hermeneutics Series. *Out of Egypt: Biblical Theology and Biblical Interpretation*, 5 vols. (Paternoster Press. 2004), pp. 146-7.

worldview paradigm or set of first principles that is different from Deism, Pantheism, Pan-en-theism or Materialism.[13]

By 'story' is not simply meant the mere recording of historical events but the actual interpretation of such events, that is, the worldview perspective or meta-theory through which a person discerns the world, existence and ultimate reality. Thus the biblical writers are not merely chroniclers of historical events but interpreters of a particular history; that is, they also inhabit a particular 'story' or worldview perspective through which they see and interpret the actual history of which they are a part. While a chronicled history is foundational for a linear understanding of the Israelite story, it is the worldview perspective of the chroniclers that is important for the meaning they assign to the chronicled history. The term 'metanarrative' will be used not merely as a reference to biblical history as chronicled by various canonical authors, but as a term that embraces their particular theistic worldview perspective, which serves as the very lens through which they interpret the Israelite covenant history.

Concepts such as the biblical covenant story or the Hebrew historical narrative do not mean that the chronological structure of the Israelite story follows the order in which the various texts are located within the canon, but that these texts implicitly and explicitly contain a historical chronology expressed by the thematic and historical markers in the text itself. Thus the Genesis narrative is thematically linked to the Exodus narrative in terms of genealogy

---

[13] For a more thorough discussion on the importance of allowing the biblical story/stories to tell the 'inside story' see Gunnar Pedersen, 'The Bible as Story' in the *Festschrift in Honour of Dr. Jan Paulsen*, eds. Borge Schantz and Reinder Bruinsma (Luneburg, Germany: Advent-Verlag, 2009), pp. 237-47. For a more general discussion of the role of worldview paradigms in human thinking see: James Sire, *The Universe next Door: A Basic Worldview Catalog*, 4th ed. (Downers Grove, IL: InterVarsity Press, 2004). See also Michael Goheen and Craig Bartholomew, *Living at the Crossroad* (London: SPCK, 2008).

and covenant promise. Whoever composed the Exodus accounts was apparently aware of the preceding covenant perspective embodied by the promise to Abraham, linking the subsequent exodus history of Israel to the preceding pre-history of creation, crisis and the remedial promise themes recorded in the Genesis account.

The critical concern is the broad chronological outlines of the emerging covenant history of Israel within which the authors appear to operate. N. T. Wright expressed the Israelite consciousness as it matured in the hopes and expectations of Second Temple Judaism by saying, 'many first-century Jews thought of the period they were living in as the continuation of a great scriptural narrative, and of the moment they themselves were in as late on within the "continuing exile" of Daniel 9.'[14] In other words they saw their covenant history as a God-directed journey extending from its perceived biblical past to its future consummation according to the biblical promise.[15] Whether this is the true story of the world is not the concern of this discourse, only the question of what kind of story the Israelite inhabited.

While there was, in the mid-twentieth century, a renewed concern for identifying levels of unity in the canon, especially within the emerging biblical theology movement of the 1950s and 1960s, the dominant trend in biblical scholarship has been towards a search for diversity and discontinuities in the biblical material rather than a search for possible levels of unity. The focus on diversity has largely been driven by the modernist deistic and naturalistic evolutionary assumptions and its assumed radical divine transcendence, a

---

[14] Tom Wright, *Justification: God's Plan and Paul's Vision* (London: SPCK, 2009), p. 42.

[15] This study does not engage in exploring the rationale for how such a history and consciousness came into being. The explanation for a deeper thematic historical unity in the Scriptural texts in terms of divine inspiration and revelation is well known, and any belief that such an explanation is the best explanation is not the focus in this study. What is the concern here is the empirical detectable evidence for such a thematic consciousness and its hermeneutic implications – not the rationale for such a consciousness.

transcendence that dominates the hermeneutics of source, form, and historical literary criticism.[16] Accordingly the idea that there is metanarrative level of unity in the scriptural narratives has been openly challenged and generally abandoned by the majority of scholars within the discipline of biblical studies.

However, for theology to be biblical it must reflect the realities of the texts in the biblical canon, including its worldview perspective. If the dominant feature of the biblical canon is diversity and discontinuity representing multiple theologies and worldviews, any attempt at detecting a unified theology is pointless. If, on the other hand, there is an ideological and thematic level of unity in the biblical material, then a biblical theology proper appears to be possible. In the emerging field of biblical theology, it is thus recognised that the Israelite covenant history represents such level of unity, when it is understood in terms of its own worldview premise, and that this provides an opportunity to formulate a methodology that could allow the Bible to tell its own story/stories on its own premises.[17] If the dominant characteristic of the biblical text is a narrative operating

---

[16] Walter C. Kaiser Jr., *Recovering the Unity of the Bible: One continuous Story, Plan and Purpose* (Grand Rapids, MI: Zondervan, 2009), pp. 11-24.

[17] The last decades have seen the emergence of a narrative approach to Biblical theology pioneered by persons like Walter C. Kaiser Jr., N. T. Wright and others. Walter C. Kaiser Jr., *Recovering the Unity of the Bible* (Grand Rapids, MI: Zondervan, 2009); Craig Bartholomew & Michael Goheen, *The Drama of Scripture* (London: SPCK, 2006), pp. ix - xii.; N. T. Wright, *Scripture and the Authority of God* (London: SPCK, 2005), pp. 89-94; N. T. Wright, *The New Testament and the People of God* (London: SPCK, 1992), pp. 121-144; T. Desmond Alexander, *From Paradise to the Promised Land* (Grand Rapids, MI: Baker Academic, 2002); *From Eden to the New Jerusalem* (Nottingham; Inter-Varsity Press, 2008); Charles H. H. Scobie, *The Ways of Our God* (Grand Rapids, MI: Eerdmans, 2003); Vaughan Roberts, *God's Big Picture, Tracing the storyline of the Bible* (Nottingham; Inter-Varsity Press, 2002); Graeme Goldsworthy, *Christ-Centred Biblical Theology, Hermeneutical foundations and principles* (Nottingham; Inter-Varsity Press, 2012).

within a theistic worldview paradigm, then such a phenomenon must be recognised in the formulation of a hermeneutics suited for retrieving the theological meaning of the biblical material. Such a hermeneutics for biblical theology could be entitled: *A Theistic Narrative Method of Biblical Theology*.

The following sections will aim at providing a methodological map outlining the hermeneutical steps needed for articulating such a unified biblical theology: firstly, to explore the triple thematic worldview perspective emerging from the Genesis story; secondly, to analyse the narrative-staged thematic characteristics of the subsequent covenant story; thirdly, to identify the transitional promise-fulfilment structure of the Scriptural covenant story and finally to examine the hermeneutical and theological implications of the apostolic principle regarding a staged fulfilment.

A Triple Meta-Narrative Persepctive

The real challenge for the biblical theology project is to recognise the nature and level of unity in the Scriptures and thus to propose a methodology that will allow the biblical texts to tell their own 'inside story' on their own thematic premises, a method that is not controlled by the worldview lenses of the interpreter. So theology, in order to qualify as biblical, must primarily be looking for the 'meaning' that is being formed by the underlying core themes of the scriptural narratives, whether such thematic perspectives are presented implicitly or stated explicitly in the texts. To dismiss or ignore such common thematic perspectives in the process of penetrating the thinking of the biblical authors would be to ignore their worldview and thus derail the attempt to uncover the theological 'meaning' of the canonical texts.

My thesis is that the canonical authors generally think in terms of a triple thematic perspective constituted by a theistic creation-theme, a deception crisis-theme and a divine redemptive-theme, a triple perspective detectable in the plot-line from the Genesis stories to the Apocalypse. If the biblical authors generally think within such a shared triple thematic horizon, they most likely inhabit a common worldview paradigm and thus share a thematic level of unity despite any diversity.

The 'Creation-Perspective' is foundational; it is located as the preamble to the entire biblical canon and apparently provides the foundational worldview horizon within which the biblical authors understand all of divine and physical time-space reality.[18] The second theme is the 'Deception Crisis-Perspective' that concerns the mysterious evil that radically disrupts the divinely intended Paradise order. The theme of human evil is central to understanding the anticipated drama expected to unfold in the human story in correlation with the double motifs regarding God's promised remedial response. The crisis perspective thus forms a constituent part of the grand universal narrative plot-line within which the various subsequent biblical sub-stories can be expected to emerge.[19]

The third theme is the dual 'Remedial Perspective' embodying the promise that God will exercise damage control, taking actions to restrain, contain and undo the evil force that now distorts human life and will simultaneously take redemptive actions to restore humans to

---

[18] The Creation Perspective. The most general, comprehensive, all-embracing and all-inclusive theory about everything encountered in the biblical material is stated up front in the Genesis preamble (Gen 1:1). There is, therefore, an implicit all-inclusive theistic principle in the Genesis formula including the derived principle of 'dependency' with regard to everything created. Accordingly, this theistic creation formula provides an all-embracing conceptual horizon or worldview paradigm.

[19] The Crisis Perspective. The second general comprehensive thematic principle embracing all of human existence encountered in the biblical material is stated up front in the Genesis preamble. (Gen 3:8-24) A cosmic and human evil is generating a state of crisis in God's plan for the world, disrupting the state of Paradise life, thus introducing a radical discontinuity in the intended story.

the Paradise life from which they are now excluded.[20] The interaction between the central crisis theme of evil and the double motifs regarding God's remedial response seems to form the grand narrative plot-line around which the subsequent story could be expected to revolve, a plot-line advancing the drama to a divinely set goal of the termination of evil and the restoration of God's intended goodness for creation embodied in the Paradise order.

In the Genesis account, the theistic first principles thus appear to provide the controlling worldview boundary *within* which the narratives are logically contained, while the theme of human evil seems to provide the centre *around* which the human-divine interaction will subsequently revolve in the time and space journey of humanity and thus as the centre around which the divinely promised remedial activity can be expected to revolve. Precisely how this human/divine drama will unfold in specific temporal stages is not developed in the Genesis account, where only the initial stages are introduced. However, the remedial promises and actions formulate the remedial principles by which the grand redemptive narrative plot-line can be expected to proceed.

My working proposal is that this threefold theological perspective, first encountered in the Genesis story (chapters 1-3), represents the paradigmatic core of the Scriptures and thus its first principles, constituting the worldview horizon within which the various authors of Scripture interpret experienced reality. The following analytical steps seem helpful in testing the proposed thesis. The first analytic task is (a) to explore and identify the basic triple thematic principles introduced in the Genesis account, and then (b) to trace to what degree and in what manner such a triple thematic principle is assumed,

---

[20] The Remedial Perspective. The biblical canon is introduced not only by a unique worldview paradigm and a central crisis theme of demonic human defiance but also by a double remedial motif with regard to God's response to the crisis of evil: a remedial response expressed in terms of the creator God's restraining curses and redemptive blessings.

maintained, deepened, applied and expanded by the various authors of the Bible, and (c) to assess to what degree the biblical 'stories' are shaped by the thematic realism of this triple worldview horizon, and finally (d) to evaluate the manner in which this triple perspective directs the advancing redemptive plot-line through the various stages of the Israelite covenant history. The next methodological step in exploring a hermeneutics for biblical theology will focus on the anticipated stages in which the drama is expected to unfold.

A Multi-Staged Narrative Structure

Some scholars[21] suggest that the biblical grand narrative divides into five or six major stages. However it could be argued that a division into seven major stages is more in line with the inner meta-narrative logic of the biblical canon seen as a whole, the latter being contingent on how the apostolic staged fulfilment principle regarding the past, present and future restorative work of the Messiah is understood. Although a major argument will not be promoted in this chapter, it seems reasonable within the apostolic eschatology to distinguish between a judgment stage and a subsequent restoration stage. These seven major stages could be defined as, *The Creation, The Crisis Event, The Hebrew Era of Promise and Exile, The Jesus Era and Fulfilment, The Gospel Era and Fulfilment, The Judgment Era and Fulfilment* and *The Restoration Era and Fulfilment*.

---

[21] N. T. Wright argues for a five-stage narrative structure while Craig Bartholomew and Michael Goheen argue for a six-stage narrative structure of the canonical master-narrative. N. T. Wright, *Scripture and the Authority of God* (London: SPCK, 2005), pp. 89-94. N. T. Wright, *The New Testament and the People of God* (London: SPCK, 1992), pp. 121-144. Craig Bartholomew and Michael Goheen, pp. ix-xii.

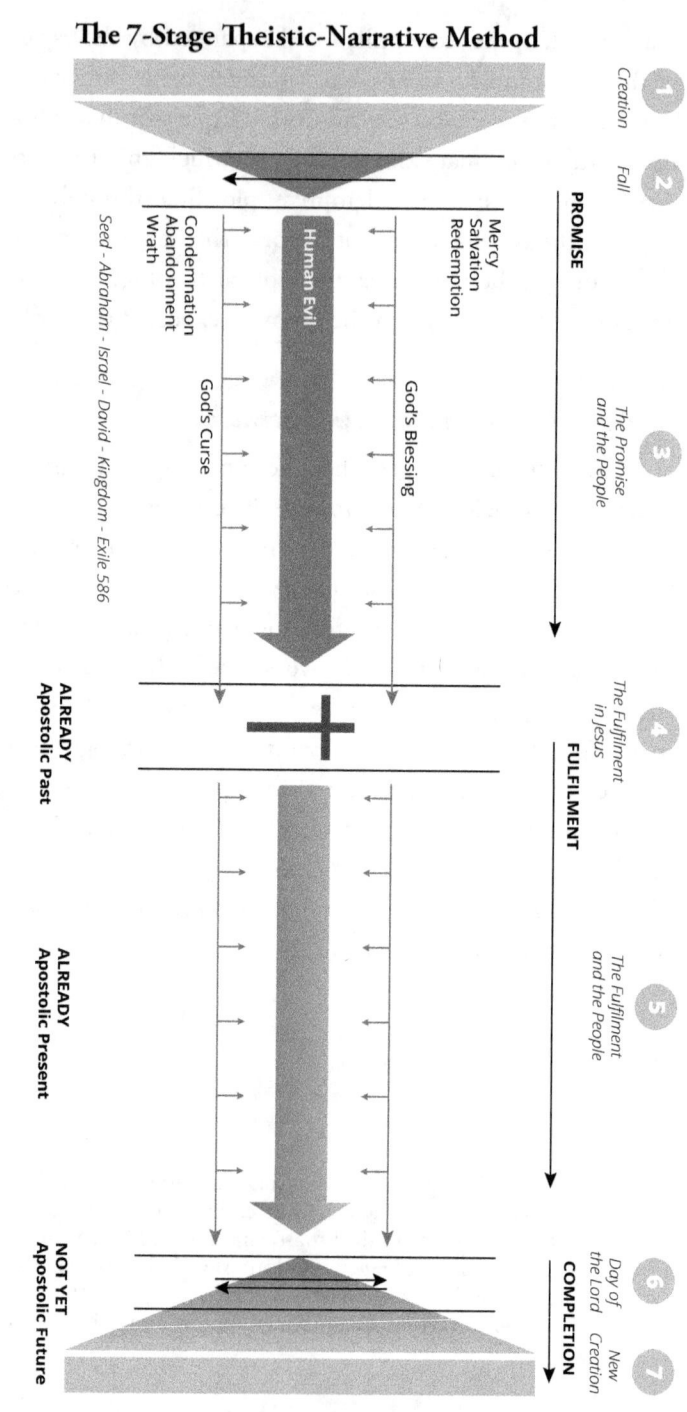

The Genesis story introduces the initial situation (Genesis 1-2) defining God's good intentions and plan and mission for the world. Then a complication and crisis (Genesis 3) is introduced followed by a string of divine remedial actions and events (Genesis 3-12) in which God is seen as taking action to remedy the new situation, actions that provide progressive temporal resolutions in anticipation of a future final resolution.

This is the narrative context in which the covenant with Abraham takes God's mission forward: a mission drama centred on God's remedial plan of blessing for the world through his descendants. The Abraham story thereby initiates the covenant narrative about Israel which focuses and structures the subsequent patriarchal history as it moves towards the promised Exodus and beyond. Further reading reveals that the remedial actions of God are only provisional in nature, being followed by a deepening crisis to be followed by further remedial actions. A repetitive expanding drama centred in the divine plan for Israel thus unfolds through the biblical stories, reaching a catastrophic climax during the demise of the Israelite kingdom and ending in destruction and exile. As the covenant history gravitates towards a catastrophic end, Israelite faith in the divine promise seems to be equally disintegrating.

This is precisely the context in which the prophets introduce a string of significant messianic-kingdom promises depicting a future 'day' when God will take decisive remedial actions to terminate the disruptive force of evil present in Israel and the world. The writings of Isaiah especially depict a grand vision, to be echoed in other exilic and post-exilic prophetic writings, of such a final solution provided by the future Messiah, the ultimate son of David, leading to the termination of the rule of evil and the restoration of a rule of goodness in the world. Prophetic literature thus proffers a string of messianic-kingdom promises that naturally generate a growing anticipation of a future era of messianic-kingdom fulfilment.

God's actions and promises, in response to the deepening crisis of evil into the late Israelite kingdom era, thus moves the Israelite meta-narrative forward stage by stage towards a major transitional event. The prophetic vision of the future messianic 'remedial acts' anticipates a future decisive transition point in the Israelite narrative, conceptually dividing the scriptural story into a two major parts characterised by a broad pattern of *'promise'* and *'fulfilment'*. This, however, does not indicate that no covenant promises have been fulfilled in the past, but that there is a significant build up to an anticipated future transitional event, when the problem of evil causing the progressive disaster will finally be resolved, and the eternal kingdom of blessing will finally be realised.

It is thus the Hebrew Scriptures themselves that anticipate the coming of a future decisive transitional stage in the advancing Israelite drama. So the real force of the apostolic proclamation is that with Jesus the decisive transition in God's mission to the world through Israel has arrived; the apostles introduce Jesus as the fulfiller of all that was promised, predicted and intended in the antecedent covenant history and they proclaim him to be the provider of the ultimate remedy to the problem of human evil. Christ is seen as graciously reconciling humans to God and renewing the human spirit before he eventually provides a restored order of things beyond the present level of human fallen existence. The apostolic understanding is, however, that this fulfilment will not be realised as a single event but rather in major successive stages broadly seen as an apostolic *'already'* and *'not yet'*. More specifically, the apostolic fulfilment scheme divides the redemptive work of Christ into the triple stages of *past, present* and *future*.[22] Thus, in the apostolic proclamation, the past and present

---

[22] The apostles from the Day of Pentecost clearly distinguish between the past, present and future restorative work of Christ, thus further clarifying that the kingdom will not be restored as a single event. Luke 19:11; Acts 2: 30-36; 3:19-21; 5:30-32; 17:30-31; Rom 2:16; 1Cor 15:20-28; 2 Tim 4:1.

work of the Messiah are embodied in the 'already' in anticipation of the 'not yet'.

The recognition of this general pattern of promise and fulfilment and the subdivisions of the fulfilment principle thus provide the reader with a major structural key to exegetical reading and doctrinal application of the Hebrew and Apostolic Scriptures. The biblical narrative is seen as proceeding in at least six major stages, of which the apostolic fulfilment story forms at least a triple temporal sequence. So if the canonical covenant story is seen as proceeding through a temporal 'already' and 'not yet' sequence, the critical hermeneutical reading issue relates to *which aspects of the promise, purpose and predictions that have already been restored, which aspects are in the process of being restored and which aspects are still to be restored as seen from an apostolic perspective.*

The narrative temporal staged nature of the emerging biblical covenant story thus has critical hermeneutical implications. Questions regarding where the various texts thematically sit in the emerging story and what constitutes their antecedent thematic context are crucial for both exegesis and application. Furthermore, the nature of the transition from promise to fulfilment signals that there will be both continuity and change in the biblical covenant story. The nature and significance of this transition is very complex and the answers given have led to deeply divergent theologies.[23] Accordingly the next section in this chapter will attempt to explore the levels of continuity and change in the Israelite covenant story before further reflecting on any hermeneutical and doctrinal implications.

---

[23] If the overarching scriptural narrative is understood as a staged journey from an earthly physical Paradise to a higher mode of existence in a heavenly Paradise beyond the present time-space reality, as is the case with various schools of Christian theology, then the central Christ event will signal the transition into a new higher heavenly mode of existence superseding and replacing the first order of creation and thus signalling a radical discontinuity within the scriptural story.

Levels of Continuity and Change

The Hebrew Scriptures clearly signal a coming transition, implying both a continuity and change in terms of the subsequent fulfilment narrative. This transition is vital for understanding which parts of the Hebrew biblical instructions are in principle provisional and which are permanent, as well as the nature and levels of changes that will transpire as the redemptive story progresses towards its promised goal. My working thesis is that with regard to the *goal* of restoration, a fundamental continuity may be observed, while on the level of the *means* of restoration, a degree of discontinuity and change may be observed. However, such a thesis is contingent on what is being understood by the goal of the covenant story and the means of its achievement. Thus the next subsection will further explore the question of the perceived goal of the Hebrew apostolic covenant story.

The Goal of Restoration

In the Hebrew covenant era there is a significant prophetic build up regarding the promises of a future restored Paradise rule of God in the world by which a permanent state of blessing is reestablished and where there will be no more evil and no more curses. The initial triple Genesis worldview perspective appears to provide the ultimate rationale for the restorative goal towards which the covenant story is moving, and thus provides the logical horizon for defining the very evil from which humans are to be saved and the goal of goodness to which humans are to be restored. Accordingly, no essential redefinition of evil and goodness is to be expected but rather a reaffirmation and a deepening exposition of the evil state that is to be eradicated and the state of goodness to be restored. So in terms of the realism of the Hebrew and Apostolic meta-narrative, redemption is seen as a restoration of God's created order.

While it is the realism of the Genesis worldview that in principle determines what has lasting validity, such as the primordial definition of good and evil, it is the crisis principle that will determine which Paradise values are being temporally accommodated in the interim crisis era, and it is the fulfilment principle that will determine which Paradise values are under restorative renewal in the 'already' of the apostolic era and which are still awaiting their full restoration in the apostolic 'not yet'.[24] On the level of redemptive achievements there is thus a progressive movement from the damage of the created order towards its future restoration, from human exclusion from the Paradise blessing to human re-entry into the intended Paradise blessing. Accordingly there is a radical continuity on the meta-narrative level regarding the character of God and his intended order for creation. However, the apostolic story also signals change and discontinuity and thus the following sub-section will attempt to explore the nature and level of such change and discontinuity.

The Means of Restoration

In the Hebrew covenant story there is a significant mosaic and prophetic build up of the themes regarding the divine remedial activities by which the problem of evil, emerging in the Genesis story, is to be overcome. Such divine remedial activities are expressed in terms of both curses and blessings, even to the point where they are institutionalised in the Israelite covenant story in the form of a civil order providing damage control and a temple order providing forgiving and renewing grace. Furthermore, the prophets increasingly

---

[24] The reading of the apostolic texts indicates that there seems to be no redefinition of the Paradise moral values to be restored and no redefinition of the demonic moral evil to be eradicated being articulated in the Ten Commandments but rather a sharpening of such values in the Christ stage of the Israelite covenant narrative. While there is evidence of accommodations of values and practices under the condition of post-Paradise life, as humans are subjected to the natural, social, spiritual curses, yet such accommodations are seen as temporary in the context of a pending promise of the removal of the curses and the future full restoration of the Paradise blessings now lost.

connect the divine remedial activities to the coming messianic king who will set up a lasting kingdom of goodness reminiscent of Paradise lost.

While the social-civil-political institutions of Israel, seen in terms of the larger crisis story, clearly appear to be a temporary measure of 'damage control', the temple provision of forgiving renewing grace clearly is seen as a 'redemptive means' for resolving the problem of human access to God. However, once the crisis problem is resolved, such remedial means would logically speaking become obsolete, as they are means to an end. However, the apostolic principle of a progressively staged fulfilment complicates the issue regarding the levels of continuity and change. The question will concern which aspects of the remedial restraint (curse) are under abolishment and which aspects of the remedial means (blessing) are under fulfilment in the apostolic and the eschatological era.

While it was anticipated in the messianic kingdom promises that the ultimate and permanent remedial activities and institutional provisions will be realised by the promised messianic fulfiller, even these final remedial provisions will, according to Jesus and the apostles, themselves become redundant when they have achieved their restorative purposes. (Matt 5:17-18; 1 Cor 15:20-28). Thus, in the logic of the biblical perspective, all remedial institutions and activities are a *means* to an end and as such, in the larger cosmic perspective, temporary in nature. Accordingly the biblical covenant narrative anticipates a discontinuity with regard to all the *means* of redemption when the goal of redemption has been accomplished.

As the apostolic fulfilment principle is applied to the *means* of restoration it is the priestly ministry of Christ, seen as the messianic arrival of the promised ultimately remedial provision, which renders the Hebrew temple ministry redundant in the apostolic 'already' of fulfilment. (Luke 24:13-49; Heb 8:1-10,34) Furthermore, it appears that it is the inauguration of Christ as the new king of Israel on the Day of Pentecost, with its re-launching of Israel as a renewed community of faith centered in Christ's rule through the Spirit, that renders the Hebrew civil political order redundant in the apostolic 'already' in the life of the community of Christ (Acts 2:30-36; 5:30-32). Both the Israelite temple ministry and civil political orders were remedial institutions and activities that God applied in the Israelite community in the pre-apostolic era. Nevertheless, the apostles recognised a deep continuity in the divine provision of grace as its redemptive purpose unfolds through the Messiah. Precisely because they saw this provision as unfolding through his person, they apparently recognised that such institutional means in the era of promise were mediatory and anticipatory of what is to come in fullness through the Messiah.

The principle of the 'already' and 'not yet' of messianic fulfilment, applied respectively to the *goal* of restoration and the *means* of restoration, thus generally indicates which elements in the Hebrew remedial institutions, practices and values have continuous validity despite temporary accommodations, and which elements will progressively discontinue and be redundant in the apostolic era of fulfilment.[25] Thus the nature and character of the Messianic apostolic transition in the Israelite covenant story has critical methodological implications for the task of proceeding from the biblical texts to theological application. Accordingly the next section will attempt to clarify further its major hermeneutical implications.

---

[25] The apostolic '*already*' and '*not yet*' fulfilment principle regarding the Hebrew promise story thus constitutes a practical hermeneutical key that determines *why* and *when* the Hebrew social and religious institutions (signs of identity, civil and temple order) will be redundant in the apostolic era and *why* and *when* the Christian social and religious institutions (signs of identity, church and Christ's priestly ministry) will be redundant in the future 'not yet' when the lost Paradise blessing is fully restored. This seems to be the hermeneutical approach of Jesus and the apostles as they read and apply the prophetic kingdom texts of the Hebrew prophets.

Hermeneutical Implications

Given the apostolic fulfilment principle, the meta-hermeneutical question relates to what aspects of God's redemptive promise, intent and purpose has been fulfilled in Christ's past redemptive work and what is being fulfilled in the apostolic present and what is still to be fulfilled in the apostolic future. The principle of the 'already' and 'not yet' of messianic fulfilment, applied respectively to the *goal* of restoration and the *means* of restoration, generally indicates which elements in the Hebrew remedial institutions, practices and values have continuous validity despite any temporary accommodations, and which elements will progressively discontinue and be made redundant in the apostolic era of fulfilment.

The continued theological doctrinal relevance or irrelevance of the scriptural themes will thus be determined by what stage in the redemptive story is inhabited by the author and reader respectively. While it is the Paradise goal of the larger biblical story that indicates what is under progressive restoration, despite any temporary accommodations, it is the stage in the covenant story that indicates what is progressively being phased out, including the means of restoration, as the restorative goals are being achieved. This logic seems to be exemplified in the reasoning of the Apostle Paul.

Apparently Paul is arguing within this fulfilment logic (Gal 3:23-29) with regard to the values to be restored and curses to be abolished. He reasons that Jesus' remedial action by his 'death' saved us from the curse. Paul argues that the curses introduced in Genesis 1-11 and incorporated in the Hebrew civil order were expressive of the temporary remedial actions by which God intended, by external disciplinary coercive means, to restrain the rule of human evil until the time and moment of the coming restoration. Paul argues that with the coming of the 'already' of the renewal it follows that the ethnic, social and gender divisions, curses incorporated into the Hebrew social and civic order, will no longer apply within the restored messianic community of Israel (2 Cor 3:7-11). This is presented by Paul as a forward step in God's restorative activities, affected by an internal renewal of the human heart by the Spirit, thus serving as an advance sign of the kind of community that is ultimately to come. This seems to be the hermeneutical logic behind Paul's concluding argument about present salvation from the curse, a curse traceable back to God's restraining orders issued in consequence of human rebellion (Gal 3:23-29).

The doctrinal applications for the community of Christ are profound, namely that within this community ethnic, class and gender divisions no longer apply. With the arrival of Pentecost, Christ through the Holy Spirit is seen as forming a new community reflecting the loving attributes of God. The divisions between Gentiles and Jews, the divisions between master and slave, and female subjection under male patriarchal supremacy are, in the larger biblical narrative, all seen as fallouts from the rule of evil; a rule to which God responds with remedial actions called curses with the intent of stabilising human and Israelite society during post-fall crisis conditions (Gen 3). None of these divine actions (curses) are expressive of God's original intent for humanity, and the abolition of such conditions is therefore part of the redemptive goal for the world as anticipated in the messianic kingdom promises.

Paul seems to apply the principle of the 'already' of restoration to the apostolic era, arguing that since God is now reordering Israel as a universal people of God, the 'sign' of circumcision ethnically dividing Israel from other peoples no longer serves a an appropriate sign for the people of God in the messianic era in which the curse of Babel is to be reversed (Gen 11:1-9). However, while ethnic, social and gender divisions are no longer applicable in the community of Christ, the curse on the natural order still remains in force, according to Paul, and will not be revoked until the final Day of restoration and glorification in the 'not yet' of fulfilment (Rom 8:18-23).

So on the level of the *goal* of the restoration of lost Paradise values, the community of Christ would in the apostolic 'already' stage of restoration be called doctrinally to participate wholeheartedly in whatever God wants restored in that era and to discontinue whatever restraining activity has been rendered redundant in that era. Likewise on the level of *means*, the community of Christ would, in the apostolic 'already' stage of restoration, be called doctrinally to proclaim the present-effective remedial activities of Christ and discontinue whatever remedial activity has been rendered redundant in that era. Furthermore, when the story eventually moves into the apostolic 'not yet' – the Day of the Lord stage – the post- apostolic community of Christ would be called doctrinally to participate wholeheartedly in whatever God wants restored during that era and to proclaim the final eschatological remedial activities of Christ. Thus the progressive promise-fulfilment story indicates what a pre-apostolic community had to believe and practice in their day, and what a community living in the apostolic 'already' have to believe and practice in their day, and what a community that will be living in the apostolic 'not yet' will have to believe and practice in their day (Dan 7:9-27; 8:9-14; Matt 24:3-12; Rev 14:6-12). Paul seems to be addressing the following hermeneutical questions: What aspects of the creation order are under restoration and what aspects of the fall order are under abolishment and what aspects of the remedial work of Christ have been fulfilled? The promise-fulfilment structure and the 'already' and 'not yet' fulfilment themes thus constitute the interpretative tools necessary for the establishment of a common meta-hermeneutics appropriate for both biblical theology and doctrinal application.

Furthermore, if the theme of God's remedial action is central to the biblical covenant story, it is not surprising that much of Scripture takes the form of narrative[26] and that the narrative appears as a

---

[26] Craig Bartholomew & Michael Goheen, Scripture & Hermeneutics Series. *Out of Egypt: Biblical Theology and Biblical Interpretation* 5 vols (Milton Keynes: Paternoster Press, 2004), p. 147.

central 'genre in the Bible'.[27] The implication is that when reading the various narrative units of the Scriptures, they should be read by tracking the themes and concepts as they thematically and logically develop towards a resolution or plot rather than reading them in the light of any later application or interpretation. Furthermore, a thematic narrative reading principle entails that one reads a narrative unit in the light not only of its internal literary thematic context, such as its inherent worldview, but also in the light of the larger antecedent thematic context that the text implicitly and explicitly assumes. Thus, it is the entire antecedent thematic context in which a given narrative unit sits that provides the basic theological setting for comprehending its meaning, regardless of any subsequent developments and applications.[28] In my proposed biblical theology project, the principles for narrative reading of the individual text are thus applied to the reading of the scriptural covenant story as a whole.

Methodologically speaking then, the thematic reading and application of any part of the canonical material would need to take into account the 'staged' location of an author/text in terms of the larger biblical covenant narrative and thus its antecedent thematic context. Furthermore, any doctrinal application must also take into account the temporal location of the reader in terms of the larger biblical narrative in order to establish what is doctrinally relevant and irrelevant according to the 'stage' in the unfolding narrative

---

[27] Craig Bartholomew & Goheen, p. 146.
[28] A narrative has a plot that is formed by the events and characters in the story as it moves from complications or crises through transformative actions leading to some resolution that may be followed by a new crisis and transformative actions leading to a new resolution. So a narrative has all or most of the following steps that must be respected in its reading and interpretation such as an initial situation, complications and crisis, transformative actions, proposed resolutions and then a temporary or final situation. The major parts of the biblical material, whether in the form of micro or macro stories, appear to fall within a narrative 'genre' as they function within the larger thematic meta-narrative perspectives of the Scriptures as a whole, that is, Creation, Crisis and Promised Resolution.

that the reader inhabits. This principle will apply both to ancient and modern readers. The above reflection provides a sketch of the meta-hermeneutical principles that could undergird a scripture-based theology, a theology beginning with *textual exegesis,* proceeding through a *thematic analysis,* ending in *systematic application.* The next and final section will provide some observations regarding such a theology.

Towards a Scripture-Based Systematic Theology

It is my proposal that a *Scripture-Based Systematic Theology* is a theology that arises from within the epistemological and hermeneutical horizon of the canonical Scriptures themselves. The argument is that meta-hermeneutical principles, such as the triple thematic worldview perspective emerging from the Genesis story, the narrative-staged thematic characteristics of the covenant story, its anticipatory promise-fulfilment structure and the theological implications of the apostolic principle of staged fulfilments, could thus yield a unified biblical theology. Such a thematic biblical theology could thus constitute the thematic bridge between textual exegesis and systematics applications. The apparent weakness of both the historical-critical and historical-grammatical methods of biblical studies is that they both fall short of detecting the interpretative significance of the meta-narrative perspectives in the biblical texts.

Irrespective of what benefits and insights may be credited to the historical-critical method[29], the weakness of this method seems rooted in its deistic naturalistic evolutionary approach, replacing and even rejecting the theistic meta-perspective of Scripture; a perspective which in our view is the key to the theological unity and meaning of Scripture and systematic applications. Thus the adoption of this interpretative model a priori rules out the interpretative significance of the meta-narrative perspectives within the biblical texts itself.

Gerald Bray comments that the rise of the 'grammatico-historical' method was a form of historical criticism reacting to the more radical 'historical-critical' approaches by avoiding the deeper philosophical issues associated with the latter. While this method does not a priori rule out the larger theistic meta-narrative perspective of Scripture, it nevertheless sidelines it with its defined focus being strictly on textual analysis, that is, the procedure of establishing the grammatical, syntactical, literary and historic meaning of the texts without engaging the text with the biblical narrative as a whole. Thus the dominant view is that doctrinal formation and application is a two step process in which systematics is either reduced to a practical summary of the empirical findings of exegesis or as the provider of the metanarrative or worldview by which the biblical material is made relevant for a contemporary reader. In summary, this method falls short of detecting the interpretative significance of the meta-narrative perspectives in the

---

[29] Craig Bartholomew and Michael Goheen, (Scripture and hermeneutics series. *Out of Egypt: Theology and Biblical Interpretation*, 5 vols (Exeter: Paternoster Press, 2004), 156. The problem with the modernist approach is, according to the two authors, its a priori philosophical positivist rejection of the entire worldview of the biblical writers and thus its search for a naturalistic explanation for the development and origin of the Bible. This approach rejects the underlying 'worldview story' of the Bible up front. They state that the biblical story is being 'held captive within the other story – the humanist narrative. And thus it will be that other story that will tend to shape our lives.' Craig Bartholomew & Michael Goheen, *The Drama of Scripture* (London: SPCK, 2006), p. 4.

biblical text itself and thus leaves it to systematics to provide its own meta-perspective for pursuing theological assessment and synthesis.³⁰

However, for dogmatic or systematics and confessional articles to be fully biblically informed, they must arise from within the field of scriptural revelation as a whole and should be controlled by its underlying meta-narrative or worldview; worldview perspectives arising from the process of the thematic analysis are defined as biblical theology. Furthermore, while biblical themes will undergo thematic developments from Genesis to Revelation, such themes may also have their natural chronological 'home' of origin at a given stage in the developing biblical covenant narrative. As each motif will be connected with a string of other biblical motifs, it will hold no independent meaning apart from the larger thematic whole of which they are all theologically a part. Even the choice of a leading doctrinal motif, in terms of hierarchically ordering a system of doctrines, should not be done randomly according to the theologian's own choice of an interpretative theory, be it derived from contemporary apologetic needs, ecclesiastical traditions or current philosophies, as such concerns could seriously distort the doctrinal formulations.

Furthermore, the major doctrinal affirmations could be 'homed' or 'stringed' in accordance with the major stages in the biblical historical narrative, starting with creation and ending in eschatology,

---

³⁰ Gerald Bray, *Biblical Interpretation Past & Present* (Downers Grove IL: IVP Academic, 1996). Gerald Bray comments that the rise of the 'grammatico-historical' method was a form of historical criticism reacting to the more radical 'historical critical' approaches by avoiding the deeper philosophical issues associated with the latter. He states that the 'mainstay of this type of criticism was textual analysis'. p. 354 Many conservative evangelicals adopted this approach. However, he notes that 'the main weakness of the grammatico-historical approach was its philosophical and theological superficiality. By effectively ruling these issues out of consideration, proponents of the method were often unable to answer the theological assertions of the more radical critics. Minute textual exegesis did not explain how the text itself had come into being, nor did it tell anyone what it meant'. p. 355.

proceeding through the redemptive stages in the mission of God and climaxing in the activities of Christ as the redemptive restorer. Doctrinal themes could thus be ordered as doctrines of origins, doctrines of crisis, doctrines of redemption – the latter being further diversified into doctrines of the 'already' and 'not yet' of Christ's restorative activities. Finally, any 'minor' doctrinal articles would naturally be located as subthemes to major doctrines from which they arise as local implications.

Finally, confessional articles could thus be articulated and taught in a more narrative shape and holistic integrated form; a form that would be significantly different from the ones arising from current contemporary pragmatic practices or those arising from the classical and philosophical traditions. Such teachings could be pre-ambled with a sketch of the biblical narrative as whole, its worldview first principles and meta-narrative assumptions, and its staged development, as a context for any extractions and applications of the relevant teachings for the post-apostolic readers. In other words, such teachings should be presented as parts of a larger biblical narrative as a whole and thus reflecting the worldview assumptions and dynamics and progression of the mission of God as it is seen as advancing towards its goal within the scriptural story.

The Church Facing Individualism
A Danish Case Study

Bjørn Ottesen

Introduction

To be true to oneself is becoming a high-ranking value in Danish society, and to find one's genuine self is for many the most important quest. The church has to relate to people who use themselves as reference points for their value system and worldview. How can the church, having Christ and the Bible as authorities, relate its message to people who approach life from so different a point of view? This chapter will discuss individualism in the pluralistic Danish society and offer some initial reflections on how the church can operate in this new environment.[1] The term individualism generally refers to the conviction that each individual has the right to experience freedom and self-realisation; that each person may pursue his or her own goals and desires and – furthermore – value independence and self-reliance. In this chapter the term is used to represent an individualistic approach to spirituality, faith and beliefs. It should not be misunderstood as referring to an egocentric lifestyle, a lack of social responsibility or disinterest in community.

---

[1] The material in this chapter further develops some parts of my DMin dissertation: Bjørn Ottesen, 'A Strategy for the Adventist Church to reach the Increasingly Secular and Postmodern Danish Population' (unpublished doctoral dissertation, Fuller Theological Seminary, 2014).

The church is always in movement just as its environment constantly changes. The overarching theme of this volume, 'ecclesia reformata semper reformanda,' implies that the church never reaches a final destination in this world. There are always new goals to reach, new ideals to strive for and new spiritual battles to fight. The statement refers not only to the internal processes in the church, but also to its mission in the world and its relationship to the society of which it is a part. The church and its leaders will constantly need to reflect on how the message of Jesus Christ and the Adventist faith relates to, and will be significant for, the people in its changing context. This chapter aspires to suggest ways in which the church can even better approach a very individualistic population typical of a Western European setting.

Background

When the Adventist[2] missionaries came to Denmark in 1878 they met a rather homogeneous population in a mainly agrarian society. Close to one hundred percent of the people were members of the national Lutheran Church through infant baptism, and had a basic understanding of fundamental Christian beliefs about God, Jesus, the Bible, the Lord's Prayer, the confessions of the church, the Ten Commandments and Christian ethics. Since then, Denmark has become a much more pluralistic society.[3] Migration, education, travel and modern media have all exposed the population to a variety of cultural and religious ideas.[4]

---

[2] 'Adventist' is used in this chapter as an abbreviated form of 'Seventh-day Adventist.'

[3] Pluralism is the coexistence of several cultural or religious expressions and identities within one population. In religion, pluralism may refer not only to the variety of religions in a society but also to the interaction between such faiths.

[4] *The Shorter Oxford Dictionary* defines pluralism as: 'The theory that the knowable world is made up of a plurality of interacting things.' *The Shorter Oxford English Dictionary: On Historical Principles.* Vol. 2 (Oxford: Oxford University Press, 2002), p. 2253.

There is a relationship between individualism and pluralism.[5] Religious pluralism in Denmark has been well documented by the *Danish Pluralism Project*[6] at Aarhus University. The Pluralism Project is an interdisciplinary research project of different humanities departments at the University. In an article published in 2012 in the *Journal of Contemporary Religion*[7] members of the research team presented data documenting a high, and increasing, degree of diversity of religion in Danish society, and a sharp increase in this heterogeneity. The national church used to have almost a 'monopoly' on religion. And, even today, over eighty percent of the population of 5.5 million people are members formally. There is, however, an increasing diversity in the national church itself, with congregations having semi-independent structures and somewhat different emphases in their theology and practice.[8] The membership of the national church is decreasing (percentage-wise), because of people leaving and immigration. The Roman Catholic Church is growing, mainly because of immigration, and now has 38,000 members. Several independent churches (including the Baptists, Methodists, Salvation

---

[5] The *Shorter Oxford Dictionary* supplies this definition of individualism: 'Self-centred feeling or conduct as a principle; a way of life in which an individual pursues his or her own ends or ideas; free and independent individual action or thought; egoism.' *The Shorter Oxford English Dictionary: On Historical Principles*. Vol. 1 (Oxford: Oxford University Press, 2002), p. 1359.

[6] Marianne C. Qvortrup Fibiger, 'The Danish Pluralism Project,' *Religion* 39/2009, no. 2 (n.a.), 169-175. This research project was begun in 2002 at Aarhus University. At first it was a study of religious groups and their adherents in the city of Aarhus, but the study has since expanded to cover the entire country of Denmark. Their homepage is: http://samtidsreligion.au.dk/en/import/csr/pluralism/

[7] Lars Ahlin et al., 'Religious Diversity and Pluralism: Empirical Data and Theoretical Reflection from the Danish Pluralism Project,' *Journal of Contemporary Religion* 27/ 2012, no. 3 (October), 403-418.

[8] Peter B. Andersen, ed., *Religion, Skole Og Kulturel Integration I Danmark Og Sverige* (Copenhagen: Denmark: Museum Tusculanum, 2006), p. 413. The report mentions a new interest among 'spiritual seekers' in engaging in pilgrimages, Christian meditation and other spiritual practices. 'Church planting' and other evangelical movements create 'alternative congregations which are more or less related to the national church.'

Army and the Adventist Church) have a few thousand members each. The Pentecostal movement in Denmark is small, compared to the situation in many neighbouring countries, with approximately 8,000 members. Over the last forty years immigration has brought many new Christian churches and groups to Denmark.[9]

The significant immigration that has taken place in Denmark over the same period has also brought several non-Christian religions to the country. Some numbers are:[10] 220,000 Muslims, 28,000 Buddhists, 12,000 Hindus, 7,000 Jews, and some alternative religious expressions such as Scientology, Theosophy and the practice of ancient Nordic religions. It is estimated that 40,000 to 50,000 people are engaged in these expressions to some degree and 6,000 to 8,000 to a high degree. The New Age 'religion' is harder to define in numbers, because its adherents operate in a more fluid way, often through centres for alternative medicine and education about a holistic lifestyle. 'It is estimated that a quarter of the adult Danish population use alternative therapies every year.'[11] These recent changes have brought many options regarding faith and worldviews to the attention of the Danes. Religion has become a menu to choose from. The individual is left with a larger responsibility than ever before, along with the freedom to make his or her own choices.

Individualism in Denmark

In this plurality individualism seems to flourish. Individualism and pluralism seem to feed into each other. Strong individualism creates a more pluralistic society and a more pluralistic society encourages more individualism. Commenting on the relationship between pluralism and individualism, Johannes Adamsen states:

---

[9] Ahlin et al., 'Religious Diversity and Pluralism: Empirical Data and Theoretical Reflection from the Danish Pluralism Project,' 407.
[10] Ibid., 407–411.
[11] Ibid., 411.

It is impossible to generalise the trends in Danish society. The very word pluralism indicates plurality. You cannot describe one new culture or one new spirituality. There are multiple cultures and multiple spiritualities in today's Danish society. The basis for pluralism is individualism. The church is therefore facing a multiplicity of different changes.[12]

Pluralism and individualism are challenges to religious organisations. Reflecting on the 'Religious and Moral Pluralism' (RAMP) research project,[13] Göran Gustafsson states that 'according to Riis, the available data now suggest that the people in the Nordic countries are prepared to view several religions as bearers of truth.'[14] Writing in another part of the same volume, Pål Ketil Botvar comments that 'the modern, specialised and pluralistic society has created a credibility crisis for religion.'[15]

Various factors have opened the way for individualism. Viggo Mortensen traces society's movement towards individualism all the way back to Martin Luther and the Reformation:

---

[12] Viggo Mortensen, ed., *Er Kristendommen under Forvandling?* (Højbjerg, Denmark: Forlaget Univers, 2005), p. 63. Steen Marqvard Rasmussen makes a similar point in another article in the same volume, 'At Tage Pluralismen Alvorligt [Taking Pluralism Seriously],' p. 87.
[13] Wilhelmus Antonius Arts and Loek Halman, *European Values at the Turn of the Millennium* (Leiden; Boston: Brill, 2004), p. 8. 'The Religious and Moral Pluralism Project, initiated by Wolfgang Jagodzinsk, is the first project aiming at investigating empirically the issue of pluralism within the domains of religion and morality. It is rooted in the Beliefs in Government project which was supported by the European Science Foundation.'
[14] Göran Gustafsson, *Folkkyrkor Och Religiös Pluralism: Den Nordiska Religiösa Modellen* (Stockholm, Sweden: Verbum, 2000), p. 30. Gustafsson refers to Ole Riis, chapter eight, on 'Pluralism in the Nordic Countries.' This volume summarises the results of research done under the name of 'Religious and Moral Pluralism' (RAMP), which is a European research project conducted in twelve countries.
[15] Ibid., p. 76. Chapter three by Pål Ketil Botvar: 'Kristen tro i Norden. Privatisering og svekkelse av religiøse dogmer. [Christian faith in the Nordic countries.]'

When Martin Luther put faithfulness to his own conscience above the laws of society and the church, he introduced a new understanding of the individual, which later in western cultural history became part of the thinking about individual human rights.[16]

Broad social movements have been at work too. In Denmark the supremacy and rule of the royal family was broken in the 1840s, thus opening the way for democracy. The national church's monopoly on religion collapsed at the same time. A new constitution was formed and signed in 1848 which guaranteed freedom of faith and worship.[17] It is not possible to trace these trends in detail within the scope of this chapter. However, it should be noted that in the aftermath of the Second World War, as Danish society prospered, the rights and independence of the individual grew stronger. Access to higher education, a strong government welfare programme, better financial conditions, women moving into the workplace and gaining more independence – all these factors gave the individual more independence with respect to his or her family, the local community, and society in general. Peter Ester notes: 'Dependence has disappeared as a condition of daily life,' as he comments on the developments in democracy, welfare and strong personal, private space.[18] He also notes: 'The social structure has been differentiated into separate, autonomous sectors: family life, work, community life, political life and church activities.'[19]

A powerful description of the move towards individualism is found in a qualitative study carried out by Inger Furseth from Norway.[20] She

---

[16] Viggo Mortensen, *Kristendommen under Forvandling* (Højbjerg, Denmark: Forlaget Univers, 2005), p. 24.
[17] Ibid., p. 25.
[18] Peter Ester, *The Individualizing Society*, 2nd ed., NUGI ; 651 (Tilburg, The Netherlands: Tilburg University Press, 1994), p. 40. In this volume, Ester reports on the EVS conducted in 1981 and 1990.
[19] Ibid.
[20] A study from Norway seems relevant to this examination of Danish culture, since these two countries are neighbours, share almost identical languages and had a common political rule for several centuries. Intermarriage and travel between the two countries are very much the norm.

interviewed in depth eight people who had grown up in three different periods of time, the 1930s to 1940s, the 1950s to 1960s and the 1980s to 1990s, with particular interest in their relationships to faith and to a faith community. The answers given in the interviews illustrate the fundamental changes that have occurred in the Nordic societies. The title of her book is in itself very telling: *From Quest for Truth to Being Oneself.* The conclusions in this doctoral study describe the three generations in very different terms. The interviewees who grew up in the 1930s and 1940s perceived the group to be an important source of identity and sense of self and they thought in terms of duty and obligations. Those who grew up in the 1950s and 1960s, however, became the generation that wanted to 'find themselves.' Rather than accepting the values and traditions passed on from earlier generations they, according to Furseth, challenged every accepted norm and explored and formed new ones, and thought in terms of 'creating their own lives.' Therefore groups were seen as entities that threaten the self. There was a change in emphasis from 'an orientation towards others to an orientation toward the self.' Interestingly, Furseth describes the youngest generation with yet other characteristics:

> In contrast to the middle-aged generation that attempted to 'find oneself,' Marianne [growing up in the 80s] takes for granted there is an inner subjective self that has true authority. For her, 'being oneself' is a fundamental concept that organises most of her ideas and experiences.... It is her subjective self that creates order in life. For Marianne, groups do not constitute a theme for conflict. If she no longer finds that a group fits her sense of self, she will simply leave it. For her, it is her subjective self that determines her religious worldviews, morality, and group membership.[21]

---

[21] Inger Furseth, *From Quest for Truth to Being Oneself* (Frankfurt am Main: Peter Lang, 2006), pp. 297-298.

This strong sense of an inner self being the true reference point for life choices and positions is confirmed in other studies. Erik Birkedal did a study of approximately 90 young people in their late teens and he concludes from his qualitative research that '... it is a widespread attitude that each individual must be allowed to believe in their [sic] own way, and not only give support to, or rejection of, a faith given or provided by others.'[22] A fundamental shift in people's relationship to religion can therefore be summarised as follows: 'The new emphasis on self implies that the post-war generation and their children only adopt these [the church's] traditions if they fit with their personal enhancement or extensions of their own selves.'[23]

A former president of the Adventist church in Denmark expressed this insight on individualism back in 2004:

> The biblical message has not been changed, but the last decades have put before us a new phase in the history of the church. As several generations in the past have passed on the 'relay baton' of truth to new generations, we have now reached a time when many must rediscover the gospel and the Adventist message, not just as a 'readymade package,' but as a result of their own seeking and finding [my translation].[24]

This statement was perceptive and caught the spirit of the times, and points to the need for an incarnational ministry. The church lives in the tension and in the creative space between Jesus and the Scriptures on the one hand, and contemporary culture on the other.

---

[22] Erling Birkedal, *Noen Ganger Tror Jeg På Gud, Men . . ?* (Trondheim, Norway: Forlaget Tapir, 2001), p. 133. A qualitative doctoral study on young people in the Norwegian national church. There are close parallels to the Danish context.

[23] Furseth, *From Quest for Truth to Being Oneself*, p. 298.

[24] Carl-David Andreasen, 'Træk Fra Formandsrapporten,' *Adventnyt* 96, no. 7/8 (2004), 9.

John Stott expressed it this way: 'The church provides the text, the world provides the context.'[25]

Similar conclusions to those above are drawn from the European Values Study (EVS)[26] by Peter Lüchau. He states that the Danes take elements from many different sources to make up their own faith and worldview. Most Danes choose to remain in the national church, since they find that their individual approach to religion can include a relationship to the church. Nevertheless, Lüchau concludes that '... the church can say whatever it wants, but the Danes will primarily listen when what is said, fits into their own private religious positions.'[27] He continues: 'In other words, the individualisation has made the Danes into members of the national church on their own terms.'[28] Religion has become a 'smorgasbord' where individuals fill their plate according to their own liking.

Individualism creates pressure both from inside and outside the Adventist church organisation. People may have grown up in the church but, nonetheless, are influenced by the individualistic society and feel less obligated to be loyal to the church, its teachings and traditions. Potential members from outside can express their liking of certain aspects of the 'Adventist message' and at the same time feel indifferent or negative towards other parts. They will not necessarily have a feeling of loyalty to an organisation. The change towards individualism seems to happen by default and the church cannot stop it. The question remains whether – and how – the church can do its

---

[25] John Stott, *Christian Mission in the Modern World* (London: Falcon, 1975), p. 29.
[26] http://www.europeanvaluesstudy.eu/. This study was done every nine years, from 1981 to 2008. This study first included eleven European countries, but that number had risen to forty-seven by 2008. It covers issues related to life, family, work, religion, politics and society. The project is mainly sponsored by the universities of the countries that participate.
[27] Lisbeth Christoffersen et al., *Fremtidens Danske Religionsmodel* (Copenhagen: Forlaget Anis, 2012), 315. Chapter Four by Peter Andersen and Peter Lüchau.
[28] Ibid., p. 316.

mission in this new setting. The Adventist church has traditionally strongly emphasised its own identity and the particulars of its message. The issue of how it can relate to the new individualistic mentality deserves more attention.

Grace Davie makes two interesting observations with regard to the relationship of people in Western Europe to the national churches in their countries. She argues that these populations are more 'unchurched' than 'secular.' She claims that for many the presence of the church has importance, even though they are not regular attendees of the church services. She notes that in times of crisis, the need for the church tends to surface. People meet in churches to find fellowship, comfort and meaning. She refers to this phenomenon in relation to the tragic circumstances of the sinking of the 'Estonia' ferry, the death of Princess Diana and the 9/11 attack in New York.[29] The other consideration is that Europeans tend to let others keep religion alive on their behalf. She introduces the concept of 'vicarious religion' and states that 'significant numbers of Europeans are content to let both church and churchgoers enact a memory on their behalf ..., more than half aware that they might need to draw on the capital at crucial times in their individual or their collective lives.'[30] These concepts seem to dovetail with the general trend that Danes want to keep their national church even though they have a rather loose relationship with it.

Closely linked to individualism is the concept of authenticity. To be true to oneself is seen by Danes as a high, even supreme, value. Furseth comments on authenticity when she writes about the move towards individualism within a Nordic context. She both defines it and remarks on its importance for different age groups.

---

[29] Grace Davie, *Europe: The Exceptional Case* (London: Darton, Longman & Todd, 2002), p. 19.
[30] Ibid.

In the stories analysed here, the discourse on authenticity centres on individual consistency between ideals and behaviour.... Whereas [those growing up in 20s and 30s] discuss individual sincerity in the area of religion in relation to one or more communities, [those growing up in the 1950s /1960s] relate these topics to the self. They operate with a notion that they have a unique, inner, authentic self where truth is to be found.... For [those growing up in the 1980s/1990s], to be genuine is related to the idea of 'being true to oneself.'[31]

Can a person be true to him-/herself and at the same time be true to Jesus Christ and to the church? Can one be authentic and still be part of a large religious community that already has agreed positions defining of what are right beliefs, opinions and correct behaviours? Many would find that impossible. It is a challenge for the church to face these questions and to create ways to meet people of different backgrounds, with strong personal positions, in forums where they can be themselves and also feel respected. The next section will attempt to give some reflection on how this could happen.

---

[31] Inger Furseth, *From Quest for Truth to Being Oneself*, p. 299.

Possible response by the church

Individualism and pluralism should not be seen only as threats to the church. They also bring opportunities. Pluralism in itself makes most people open-minded and – often – interested in the opinions of others. Today people are not stigmatised for being Christians and belonging to a church, as they tended to be in the 1970s and 1980s. An attitude of curiosity among people in general provides an opening for the gospel.

Interestingly, the Adventist Church came into being because its pioneers were individualists who dared to stand out from the crowd and hold unorthodox positions. A crucial difference, however, is that they sought truth in the Scriptures whereas many today see their inner being as their main point of reference. Can the Adventist Church handle the individualists in its midst today? Can a traditional church model accommodate this new mentality, or is there a need for a more flexible approach to membership and belonging in Adventist churches? In most Adventist contexts one becomes a member and belongs when one has accepted a series of doctrines, a particular lifestyle and certain behaviours. If belonging is so closely tied to consent and assimilation, it will easily clash with the strong value of autonomy and individuality that most people cherish. Is there a third way between uniformity and total individualism?

In the remaining sections let me present some perspectives suggesting a way forward for the church as it seeks to connect with and engage people in an individualistic society. These reflections on relationships, belonging and membership, might differ somewhat from the general thinking in Adventist churches, but could hopefully be helpful in the church's mission. The first reflection is on something as simple as venues. Church buildings tend to represent an establishment with set doctrines and set behaviours; an organisation that has ready-made answers, but does not listen to the individual or accept their differing point of view. That clashes with the very mentality of the individualistic person. Research by the Lutheran National Church in Sweden in the 1990s sought to discover what existential questions people were interested in, and in what context they would like to discuss these questions. With regard to what context was good for such dialogues, 62 percent said they would like to discuss existential matters 'with one or a few of their friends' and 21 percent answered that they wanted to meet in 'a small informal group in a home,' a total of 83 percent. Only 8 percent (these being women only) answered that they could see themselves discussing these issues in a 'church building.'[32] In an individualistic society each person expects to be listened to and that their opinions will be valued as highly as any other. For many this seems impossible in a setting where beliefs and lifestyle are already defined. Forums have to be established where there is an atmosphere of trust, liberty for all to express themselves, respect for everyone's opinion, a sense of equality and commitment to the group. Neutral places like community centres, cafés, libraries or homes signal that all meet on equal terms. More on this below.

A second reflection relates to how the church communicates its message. The individualistic mentality challenges the traditional programmes of the church and to some degree the existence of the central organisation. The individualist, who considers himself or herself to be the reference point, does not come to a community only to listen, but also to be heard and to test out ideas with others. No one is seen to have more authority than another. People want a dialogue that gives all parties equal standing and input. The popularity of blogs, phone-in programmes and the like demonstrate the importance of a two-way exchange and the democratisation of ideas in today's world. This spills over to issues of spirituality. This leads to a clash of cultures as the programmes in the church are usually designed to promote the ideas of the institution. Worship services invite participation in

---

[32] Rolf Gustafson, *Tid För Dialog* [Time for Dialogue] (Uppsala: Trotts Allt, 1994), p. 37.

singing and praying, but do not open the door for an exchange of ideas. The one-way communication of the sermon is not used in many other forums in society. In news services, talk shows and even classrooms, people are presented with various points of view, and each person is encouraged to form a personal opinion. The church needs to think hard about what forum it will create for discussions that are open-ended. Most Adventist churches have a Bible study hour before the 'divine service' every Saturday (Sabbath school). This is potentially a very good opportunity for dialogue. However, the traditional Bible study guides seem rigid to a questioning mind. The study guides are usually designed with questions, followed by one or two Bible passages and an explanatory paragraph which gives the answer to the questions. This style does not encourage independent thinking and is far different from the teaching methods used in school classrooms or in universities. Even public church meetings have generally followed the model of monologues and the delivery of information.

The Adventist Church does not necessarily have to change its doctrines to develop a different profile,[33] but it needs to state its *raison*

---

[33] George Knight, an Adventist historian quoted throughout Chapter 5, discusses this in *The Neutering of Adventism*. George R Knight, *The Apocalyptic Vision and the Neutering of Adventism* (Hagerstown, MD: Review and Herald, 2008). His first argument is that the Adventist Church needs to have a stronger focus on Christ and the Gospel of grace. But he also states that if the Adventist Church forgets its particular doctrines and its prophetic message, it will lose its identity and thereby its reason for existence. That is probably true if one is speaking about a Christian society, but in relation to a spiritual seeker in Danish society the church will probably find its strength in providing meaning, resources for spiritual growth and worthwhile principles and values to live by. The church will still be able to maintain its doctrines, but that will not be the main focus in its initial contact with seekers.

d'être in a life-affirming way,³⁴ helping people to discover meaning for their lives, find spiritual values and provide them with opportunities to put these into practice in real relationships. The church would profit from considering how it can provide room for individuals to find their own paths forward. Many are looking for a framework of thought, values and lifestyle that gives guidance to their lives. The Adventist Church can provide such a framework, but it is better presented as an offer than a 'straitjacket.'

The third reflection relates to membership and a sense of belonging. Adrian Peck did two case studies in England,³⁵ describing two growing local churches: Christ Church London and Kingsgate Community church in Peterborough. He observed a philosophy of ministry and church government that demonstrated the difference between a 'center set' or a 'bounded set' conception of church. The terminology comes from anthropologist Paul Hiebert. A group using the "bounded set" model would define belonging as adhering to certain beliefs and behaviours. Those who comply with these would be seen as being 'inside' and being part of 'us' as opposed to those who think or act differently who would be regarded as 'outside' and 'them'. Beliefs and behaviours become a fence defining who is 'in' or 'out.'

> ...[A] centre set model as being based on 'intrinsic rather than extrinsic characteristics,' such that one's

---

[34] The present world leadership puts a lot of emphasis on the particular Adventist doctrines which were formulated in the 1800s. That has its place, but these formulations do not necessarily speak to the needs of the Northern European. The emphasis on doctrines has been strong in many public presentations and been transmitted widely. Two examples would be the first sermon of the world leader after his election (http://www.youtube.com/playlist?list=PLB72DA3F3193CCC16) and his speech at the annual council in 2010 (http://www.youtube.com/watch?v=NqxzN8rdSC8). The church needs to bring forward some of its more practical contributions to personal life and the community, how it can help each individual on their journey through life, and the spiritual aspects of the Christian walk.

[35] Peck, Adrian, 'Church Growth In Britain: A Thematic Analysis of Two Growing British churches.' (Unpublished MA thesis, Newbold College: 2014). See, in particular, chapter 7, 80-95.

relationship to a defined centre, based on movement away or towards that centre, determines whether a person is a member of the set. This is not a boundary free system as there is a clear division between things moving in and those moving out. For a church the centre is Jesus.[36]

In the centre set model, individuals' standing is defined by what direction they are moving in, not how far from, or close, they are to the centre. In the sample churches, belonging was defined by a movement towards the centre: Christ, the gospel and the basic values of the kingdom of God as outlined by Jesus. These churches had created a vocabulary and simple rituals to acknowledge and affirm a person's belonging and commitment – even if he/she was not a formal member. These churches also had 'levels' of membership indicating levels of involvement in that particular local church, but these categories were not defining a person as 'in' or 'out.' Involvement in church ministries was open to non-members and served as another factor to confirm belonging. The Adventist church in Europe might profit from doing some rethinking about the vocabulary we use for members and others in order to reflect an inclusive spirit. Language carries values. Furthermore it is worth rethinking the path into membership, particularly as this process of joining the church is taking longer and longer for the average person. To confirm a new believer's steps towards faith in Christ and towards membership e.g. in a public ritual, would create a sense of belonging, although a formal

---

[36] Peck, Adrian, 'Church Growth In Britain,' 80, referring to Paul G. Hiebert, 'The Category "Christian" in the Mission Task,' *International Review of Mission*, 72 (1983), 423. Paul Hiebert was the first person who applied social set theory to churches. The same focus is expressed by Frost and Hirsch. They speak about an 'ecclesiology entirely on missional grounds,' which is incarnational rather than attractional, so that the church becomes 'instinctively centrifugal, and not centripetal.' See Michael Frost and Alan Hirsch, *The Shaping of Things to Come: Innovation and Mission for the 21st-Century church* (Peabody, MA: Hendrickson Publishers, 2003), xi, 12, 41.

membership and even baptism was not yet an option. The church has to recognise that individuals generally do not want to be swallowed up into an institution, but want to be part of the group on their own terms and moving at their own pace.

Fourthly, as entry points into Christian fellowship, Adventist churches might consider using other forums than Sabbath morning services and Sabbath School meetings, which tend to target 'insiders' and take agreement to Adventist doctrine for granted. Some churches have experimented with that and have found small groups in homes a 'neutral' place for spiritual growth.[37] These informal settings allow for people to develop at their own speed according to personal choices. The Café Church in Copenhagen had a strong small group ministry in its early years and in those groups people grew according to their own pace and the leading of the Holy Spirit. The Café Church was very strategic about building relationships inside and outside the church. Most visitors were friends, colleagues and acquaintances of people already attending, and in that way they had a connection to the church beyond the programme itself. Many church services ended with small group discussions on the sermon topic. This was easily achieved because the church was furnished with small round tables and circles of chairs. This was an introduction to house groups which all were encouraged to attend. Rebecca Pedersen recalls that out of

---

[37] The information below comes from in-depth interviews with leaders in the respective churches. The interviewees from the Café Church in Copenhagen were Susanne Wiik Kalvaag (member from the early beginnings and at present worship leader – SK), Cyril Kalvaag (member from the start and currently elder – CK), and Rebecca Pedersen (member from early in the Café Church history and small group leader from 1999 to 2004, currently pastoring a different church plant – RP). SK and CK were interviewed together by the author via Skype from Fredensborg, Denmark, 21 August, 2013. RP was interviewed in person by the author in Bracknell, England, 6 September, 2013. The group interview with the leadership team from X-preszo, Rotterdam included people who have been in the church plant from the start – or very close to that: Martin Altink (AT), Marco Bervoets, Renate Hazel (RH), Steven Hazel (leader, SH), Esther van de Putte (EP), Paul van Putten, and Alexander Trueman. Interview led by the author at Huis ter Heide, the Netherlands, 25 August, 2013.

approximately 120 visitors, 85 attended a house group. Stronger bonding, spiritual growth and discipleship took place in the groups which had relevant materials, focused leadership, and strategic plans. Cyril Kalvaag mentioned the strong individualism that people brought to the groups, but also that praying and reading the Bible created 'the question in their own mind as to whether they are the central shaft around which the universe is turning.... People meet God in prayer.' In the context of the Café Church the small groups did not bring many new visitors to the church, but established them in the community and helped them to grow.

Another example, outside Denmark, is X-preszo in Rotterdam which started with 'Matthew-parties' rather than church services. A Matthew-party takes its model from the disciple who invited his friends to a party where they could meet Jesus (Luke 5:27-32). From that philosophy the church started with barbeques, games in the park and other social events for their friends and the community in general. According to Steven Hazel people came just to 'hang out' and expressed appreciation for the fellowship and fun; '... you are good people. I want to be with you.' The fellowship in the Matthew-parties was not based on a common religious conviction. Anybody was welcome. 'People want to belong, to be included.' The strong emphasis on building community, regardless of faith issues, can be illustrated by key words the leadership team used to describe their church: food, relevance, authenticity, attention, friendship, and acceptance. Renate Hazel concluded the little brainstorm session with the exclamation 'We accept people as they are – with everything they have. We care.'

This open attitude also characterised the profile of the house fellowships related to X-preszo, which were named 'life groups' because all aspects of life could be talked about. There was 'sharing, laughing and crying.' Individuals were welcomed on their own terms and were not pushed into a programme or a faith. Some grew into the

Christian faith, some did not. This open atmosphere was carried along as X-preszo started worship services. After some initial adjustments, X-preszo has continued its Matthew parties and connected these to their worship time. 'Some come and hang out. Some are attracted to the spiritual content; some are not.... We make room for Jesus to do what he does by being relaxed and being ourselves' (RH).

In addition to introducing new forums for people to encounter the Adventist Christian faith, these two examples introduce a final reflection: Spiritual growth happens in relationships – under the guidance of the Holy Spirit. It is not a cleverly designed programme, strategic advertising, the best speaker or wonderful facilities that result in spiritual growth for the individualistic European. People are gradually changed when they live in relationships with real people, honestly sharing life's struggles, and where prayer, Bible study and personal reflection is taking place in an authentic way. They need to be given space, to be accepted as they are and must share in the challenge of what it means to be under the influence of the Holy Spirit and the Word of God.

Conclusions

The church must duly consider the individualistic mentality in our society as it reflects on the mission God has given to the church. This is how people are. The church should approach its task with its audience in mind. This is part of 'Ecclesia reformata semper reformanda.' The Christian community must 'reform' itself in view of the mission task and the community in which it serves. This is not necessarily easy and might prove painful for the community, as is usually the case with change. Even in the Scriptures we read of changes which were painful and took a lot of courage to implement. When Israel had to establish new worship practices in captivity without the institutions of the temple, the priests and the sacrifices, it was a time of difficult adjustment. When the early church moved from being a Jewish sect in Jerusalem and Judea to becoming an international movement which accepted people of many cultures with different lifestyles and practices into its fellowship, it was highly controversial and conflict followed. For the Adventist church to respond to a new mentality, a spirit of reform and willingness to change is necessary. The tensions, frustrations and misunderstandings that might follow will be part of the leadership challenge. For example, to redefine membership, give individuals more space for personal growth or to have a looser organisations with a high emphasis on house groups and relationship – all seem to challenge traditional patterns. Questions arise on practical, organisational and theological arenas; Adventist identity, purity of doctrine, who can be involved in ministry and Adventist thinking about 'us' and 'them' are issues that will demand answers.

This chapter has demonstrated that individualism is a strong aspect of Danish (European) identity. Somehow the church needs to bring an understanding of this phenomenon into its mission strategy and evangelistic thinking. Individualists can find faith, fellowship, and belonging and grow into spiritual maturity if they are given the space they need by the Christian community.

Being Content with Ishmael
A Sermon on Learning from Abraham's Experience of Learning and Unlearning

Laurence A. Turner

I have spent almost half a lifetime teaching for the church. Recently, I have been asking myself some simple but searching questions. Such as, 'Over all of that time, what did I learn? And what have I had to unlearn?' On this matter of what we have to learn and what we have to unlearn, it is always worth turning to Scripture. Out of many places we could go, I have chosen the story of Abraham. What does Abraham have to learn and what does he have to unlearn?

All of us, as theology teachers, know the difficulty of coming to a familiar biblical narrative. We already know the end of the story. But, of course, Abraham did not know the end from the beginning. So, let us come to this story, as far as it is possible, as first-time readers. That is, let us try to experience this story, as Abraham did, in real time. And the reason for doing this? So that we can see more clearly what Abraham had to learn. And what he had to unlearn.

His story starts off in Gen 12:1-3.

> Now the LORD said to Abram, 'Go from your country and your kindred and your father's house to the land that I will show you. I will make of you a great nation, and I will bless you, and make your name great, so that you will be a blessing. I will bless those

who bless you, and the one who curses you I will curse; and in you all the families of the earth shall be blessed.

There is a lot in those three verses – too much for us to consider in only one sermon. So let us look at this one representative detail. 'I will make of you a great nation' (v. 2a).

In his understanding of what God wants in his life, here is Abraham's *major learning experience no. 1*.

So, that is clear then. Abraham, for the first time, learns he will become a great nation. But contrary to popular opinion, this story is clear and straightforward only if we read it from hindsight. It is only clear and straightforward if we don't see that Abraham had many things to learn and many, many things to unlearn.

When Abraham learns that he will become the father of a great nation, he knows something and we know something. 'Now Sarai was barren; she had no child' (Gen 11:30). So when he learns that he will be the father of a great nation, he knows and we know two things: first, Sarai his wife is barren and second, he will become a great nation. God says absolutely nothing about Sarai conceiving a child. There are possibly many ways Abraham will become a great nation, but sadly, apparently not by having a child with Sarai. For, Sarai is barren and God does not promise her a child.

So then, how is Abraham to become a great nation? More to the point, how does *Abraham* think he might become a great nation? Well, as we all know, biblical narratives are famously reserved in what they tell us about characters' motives. In most cases we need to read between the lines. So, consider this. 'Now the LORD said to Abram, "Go from your country and your kindred and your father's house to the land that I will show you"' (Gen 12:1). Abraham is told to leave his relatives. But he takes Lot with him. And who is Lot? He is his dead brother's son; his nephew. So, God tells him 'Leave behind your relatives', and Abraham takes his nephew. Doesn't that strike you as a bit odd? Especially since the Hebrew text makes it clear that Abraham left his father behind. According to the Hebrew text, Terah lived for another 65 years after Abraham left.[1] So God tells him, 'Leave your relatives', and he leaves his father. But he takes his nephew. Abraham, the man with no child takes the child who has no father. Might this suggest that Abraham sees Lot as more than his orphaned nephew, and more as a surrogate son? The one possibly through whom the great nation will come?

Consider the following. 'Then the LORD appeared to Abram, and said, "To your offspring I will give this land." So he built there an altar to the LORD, who had appeared to him' (Gen 12:7). God promises the land to Abraham's descendants. And not long afterwards Abraham says this to Lot, 'Is not the whole land before you? Separate yourself from me. If you take the left hand, then I will go to the right; or if you take the right hand, then I will go to the left' (Gen 13:9). Abraham appears to be dividing the land – promised to Abraham's seed, remember – between himself and Lot. No sooner has that happened than Lot is captured by foreign kings. And as soon as he hears, Abraham gathers his men together, gets on the battlefield and rescues Lot from those foreign kings. Abraham risks his life for Lot. So, at the very least, Lot seems to be very important to Abraham. In fact Lot seems to be more important to him than Sarai. For Abraham did nothing to rescue *her* from a foreign king in Egypt.

By the time we get to Genesis 15 we meet a passage with corrupt Hebrew. I could, but I will not, delay you with the details of the lacunae and *hapax legomena*. So, let us focus on what is clear: '... no

---

[1] If Terah is 70 years old at Abraham's birth (11:26), when Abraham leaves Haran at the age of 75 (12:4), then Terah would be 145. Yet Terah dies aged 205 (11:32). The Samaritan Pentateuch gives Terah's final age as 145. Presumably, this is the tradition known to Stephen in Acts 7:4, where he says, 'After [Abraham's] father died, God had him move from there to this country.' Ellen White also reflects this tradition (PP 127). Despite attempts to argue otherwise, the Hebrew chronology presumed in this sermon is clear in the text.

one but your very own issue shall be your heir' (Gen 15:4b). Here, for the first time, Abraham learns that he will father a child. And his own flesh and blood will become a great nation.

So then, major learning experience no. 2. God says to Abraham, 'About the promise Abraham – try looking at it this way'. The great nation will not come through Lot (or through the enigmatic Eliezer of Damascus). Abraham must be the biological father of the child of promise.

So, that is clear then. Then, we're reminded of something. 'Now Sarai, Abram's wife, bore him no children' (Gen 16:1). We already know this. But this is no redundant repetition. The purpose of repeating it is this. While Abraham *must* be the father of this child, Sarai *cannot*. For, she is barren and God has said nothing – absolutely nothing – about Sarai having a child. So Sarai introduces her husband to her Egyptian servant-girl Hagar. And the rest, as they say, is history. 'Hagar bore Abram a son; and Abram named his son, whom Hagar bore, Ishmael' (Gen 16:15). And there you have it, just as the Lord had promised. Abraham must father a child. And he does. Praise be to God for his leading. Ishmael must be the child of promise. So that is clear then.

Abraham has just settled down to this blissful truth, when the Lord says to him, 'About the promise Abraham – try looking at it this way': 'As for Sarai your wife, you shall not call her Sarai, but Sarah shall be her name. I will bless her, and moreover I will give you a son by her. I will bless her, and she shall give rise to nations; kings of peoples shall come from her' (Gen 17:15-16). And Abraham answers, 'Sarah? You never said anything about Sarah!' He has never heard this before. It is so preposterous that he falls flat on his face and laughs. And then comes the most telling statement of all. 'And Abraham said to God, "O that Ishmael might live in your sight!"' (Gen 17:18). Abraham is content with Ishmael. He has been willing to learn this and learn that. But he does not want to unlearn *this*. This is Abraham's Ishmael moment.

So, major learning experience no. 3. The great nation will not come through Lot, his adopted son. Nor will it come through Ishmael, his biological son. The child of promise will come from the union of Abraham and Sarah. So, that is clear then.

Sarah is crucial. For the first time Abraham learns that. So, why in the world do we read next, 'From there Abraham journeyed toward the region of the Negeb, and settled between Kadesh and Shur. While residing in Gerar as an alien, Abraham said of his wife Sarah, "She is my sister." And King Abimelech of Gerar sent and took Sarah' (Gen 20:1-2). Why does he risk losing Sarah? Now of course he has done it before. He did back in Genesis 12 when they first went down to Egypt. But it gets worse. Abraham has a habit of doing this. A very long habit, apparently. 'And when God caused me to wander from my father's house, I said to her, "This is the kindness you must do me: *at every place to which we come*, say of me, He is my brother"' (Gen 20:13). All of that might be understandable, if morally questionable, when Abraham did not know the importance of Sarah. *But now he does*. And he is still doing it! Does Abraham really believe the promise? Is he still living out his Ishmael moment? 'Oh that Ishmael might live in your sight!'

Yet all of these twists and turns in the plot appear to come to their end with this announcement: 'The LORD dealt with Sarah as he had said, and the LORD did for Sarah as he had promised. Sarah conceived and bore Abraham a son in his old age, at the time of which God had spoken to him' (Gen. 21:1-2). At last, we seem to reach the fulfilment of the promise. All the elements match. Abraham the father – check. Sarah the mother – check. A son born to both of them – check. Everything lines up. All of God's stated conditions are fulfilled. This whole story has come to its climax. So, that is clear then.

Until major learning experience no. 4. 'After these things God tested Abraham. He said to him, "Abraham!" And he said, "Here I am." He said, "Take your son, your only son Isaac, whom you love, and go to the land of Moriah, and offer him there as a burnt offering on one of the mountains that I shall show you"' (Gen 22:1–2). After *these* things. What things? Well, after *these* things: apparently trusting in Lot as his heir; being content with Ishmael as his heir; persistently passing off Sarah as his sister. And a whole lot more. After *these* things. That is why there is the need to test Abraham. And what is the result of the test? 'He said, "Do not lay your hand on the boy or do anything to him; for now I know that you fear God, since you have not withheld your son, your only son, from me"' (Gen 22:12). '*Now* I know.' That is, before this there was room to doubt. In this story, not only does Abraham have to repeatedly learn and unlearn. It seems even God himself learns something about Abraham too.

Now let us pay a visit to Abraham after he has returned from Mount Moriah. We approach his tent during the heat of the day. He prepares food and drink for us. And as we eat together one of us asks, 'So Abraham, have you learned anything recently?' And he says, 'Learned anything? Well, where do I begin? I might as well start with Sarah. You know, I thought that was clear enough. No hope of her having a child. She had no part to play at all. And then I discover, she is just as important as I am for fulfilling the promise. The person I thought was least significant is actually the most significant. I think they call that 'grace'.

'And another thing. I've learned that God doesn't reveal everything at once. He fed me new information, one piece at a time. I know that God has been patient with me. But, now I see that I need to be patient with God. I jumped to conclusions. And some of the things I did, like Ishmael, threatened the very promise I thought I was helping.

'And another thing, I was better at preservation than I was at innovation. I thought that each step of the way with God was the final step. That is what I meant when I said, "O that Ishmael might live in your sight!" I wanted to preserve what I had. I was content with Ishmael. That experience made me learn that the life of faith needs to be creative; pushing the boundaries, taking risks; being willing to move on with God.'

So, that is clear then. And listening to Abraham, as theology teachers employed by the church, we could well ask, 'Have we had any Ishmael moments recently?' Preservation rather than innovation? Sometimes, when I am in a mischievous mood, I ask people this question. 'What do you think are the three most exciting theological innovations in Adventism over the last twenty years?' The responses vary, but what they amount to is, 'That's an interesting question. I'll get back to you.' I would say that one of the greatest dangers for us as Adventist theologians is to see ourselves as preservers of the past rather than innovators for the present and future. For, in my opinion, theology should be a creative discipline, if indeed we believe the Lord has new things to bring forth from his word. And if theological innovation is going to happen in our church, one would hope we would be at the forefront of that. Unless we're content with Ishmael, that is.

At graduation weekend at the conclusion of my first year of teaching in Australia I was given the honour of speaking at the Friday night meeting. While I was expounding the word of God to the saints, in the car park a group known as the 'concerned brethren' were distributing flyers under the windscreen wipers, denouncing the dangerously heretical new lecturer from England. My sin? They had procured a copy of a student's essay on Daniel. I had given him a very high mark, and commended him for his 'innovative approach to the text'. But as the concerned brethren said, 'We don't want innovation. We just want the pillars of the faith.' That we need the pillars of the faith none of us would deny. But the pillars of the faith without innovation? That is being content with Ishmael.

The Tate Gallery in London is one of the UK's premier art galleries. From its foundation in 1897 it arranged its exhibits in thematic displays. People admired the works of art but got no coherent narrative of British art. Then in 2013 there was a rethink. Rather than hanging the exhibits thematically, they were rehung *chronologically*. Exactly the same exhibits, but rearranged. And the result? A totally different narrative emerged. For, each work of art is now in a different context than before. The rehang has been called 'triumphant'; 'gloriously satisfying'; 'unexpectedly beautiful'.[2] As we consider the story of Abraham, it seems that God was periodically rehanging the exhibits. Saying, 'About the promise Abraham – try looking at it this way. My promise hasn't changed. That remains the same. But if you consider this, I think you'll have a very different understanding of it.'

And my point is …? My point is that it is time to rehang Adventism. Rehang it so that it is more obviously centred on Christ. So that those who never give it a second thought now could say that it is, 'triumphant'; 'gloriously satisfying'; 'unexpectedly beautiful'. And how might we rehang the Adventist gallery? Try looking at it this way.

Move Creation from contentious arguments and rehang it between social responsibility and Christian joy. Move the Sabbath from legal obligation and rehang it between justice and celebration. Move the Second Coming from dry apocalyptic calculations and rehang it between hope and trust. Move the Scriptures from theological controversy and rehang them between imagination and wonder. That is, learn how to rethink Adventism. Just as Abraham had major learning adjustments to make as God led him to the fulfilment of his promise, so we might need to embrace major learning adjustments as God leads us to the fulfilment of our promise, the advent hope. That is, like Abraham, we need to learn how not to be content with Ishmael.

---

[2] http://www.bbc.co.uk/news/entertainment-arts-22522101

For Further Reading

Bakhos, Carol, 'Abraham Visits Ishmael: A Revisit', *Journal for the Study of Judaism in the Persian, Hellenistic and Roman Period*, 38 (2007), 553-80.

―――, *Ishmael on the Border: Rabbinic Portrayals of the First Arab* (Albany, NY: State University of New York Press, 2006)

Cohen, Aryeh, 'Hagar and Ishmael: A Commentary', *Interpretation*, 68 (2014), 247-56

Heard, R. Christopher, 'On the Road to Paran: Toward a Christian Perspective on Hagar and Ishmael', *Interpretation*, 68 (2014), 270-85.

Sherwood, Yvonne, 'Hagar and Ishmael: The Reception of Expulsion', *Interpretation*, 68 (2014), 286-304.

Turner, Laurence A., *Genesis*, Readings: A New Biblical Commentary, 2nd ed. (Sheffield: Sheffield Phoenix Press, 2009), pp. 57-82.

―――, 'Genesis, Book of', in *Dictionary of the Old Testament: Pentateuch*, ed. by D. W. Baker and T. Desmond Alexander (Downers Grove, IL: Inter-Varsity Press, 2003), pp. 350-59.

www.ingramcontent.com/pod-product-compliance
Lightning Source LLC
Chambersburg PA
CBHW052133010526
44113CB00035B/2116